IN THE SHADOW OF THE GREAT WAR

IN THE SHADOW OF THE GREAT WAR

The Milligan and Hart Explorations of Northeastern British Columbia 1913–14

JAY SHERWOOD

ROYAL **BC** MUSEUM
Victoria, Canada

Published by the Royal BC Museum, 675 Belleville Street, Victoria, British Columbia, V8W 9W2, Canada.

All photographs by G.B. Milligan unless stated otherwise in the caption. Copyright or reproduction rights remain with the source credited in the caption. All images reprinted with permission.

BCA = Royal BC Museum, BC Archives.

CVA = City of Vancouver Archives.

LTSA = Land Title Survey Authority, Victoria. (All LTSA images are from file 7919, unless stated otherwise.)

NMAI = National Museum of the American Indian, Smithsonian Institution, Washington, DC.

RBCM = Royal BC Museum, Ethnology Collection.

Edited, produced and typeset (in Bembo Std 11/13) by Gerry Truscott, with editorial assistance from Amy Reiswig.

Cover design by Stuart Wootton, form-creative.ca.

Index by Carol Hamill.

Printed in Canada by Friesens.

Library and Archives Canada Cataloguing in Publication

Sherwood, Jay, 1947–

   In the shadow of the Great War: the Milligan and Hart explorations of northeastern British Columbia 1913–1914 / Jay Sherwood.

Includes bibliographical references and index.
ISBN 978-0-7726-6637-6

   1. Surveying – British Columbia, Northern – History. 2. British Columbia, Northern – History – 1871–1918. 3. Surveyors – Canada – Biography. 4. Milligan, George Berry, 1888 July 9-1918 March 24. 5. Hart, E.B. I. Royal BC Museum II. Title. III. Title: Milligan and Hart explorations of northeastern British Columbia 1913–1914.

FC3824.9 S53 2013   971.1'803   C2013-980056-5

Contents

To Lil McIntosh (1916–2012).
Her friendship, her interest in the history of British Columbia's central interior and her years of volunteer work with the Nechako Valley Historical Society inspired me to write history books.

And to the First Nations people who assisted Milligan and Hart in their explorations.

Introduction

In 1913 the government of British Columbia issued contracts for two small but significant surveying explorations in the far northeastern part of the province. Both lasted for 18 months and were the first provincial surveying expeditions where the men remained in the field for more than a year. Both crews wintered at the small Hudson's Bay Company post at Fort Nelson, where almost everyone, including the priest, had to snare rabbits to forestall starvation. The centennial of these explorations is an excellent opportunity to recount these two important but largely overlooked adventures in the history of British Columbia.

The years before World War I were the golden age of surveying in British Columbia. From 1909 to 1913, the provincial government spent more than four per cent of its budget on surveying. From 1910 to 1914, 147 surveyors received their BC land surveying commission – it would take another 39 years for the next 147 commissions. Many surveyors worked on government contracts in a variety of projects related to agriculture, forestry, mining and transportation. The majority of these projects were in central and northern BC. Initially there were many surveys related to the construction of the Grand Trunk Pacific and the Canadian Northern railways.

In 1912 the government began to focus more attention on surveys in the far northern part of the province. Frank Swannell (PLS #75★), a prominent Victorian who had done lot surveys for agriculture in the Nechako River valley from 1908 to 1911, received a contract to do an exploratory survey of the area north of Fort St James. By surveying from mountain tops and

---

★ Provincial Land Surveyor, the designation given to a surveyor licensed by the government of British Columbia from 1891 to 1905. Since 1905 all registered land surveyors in the province have been designated British Columbia Land Surveyor (BCLS). Numbers are assigned in chronological order.

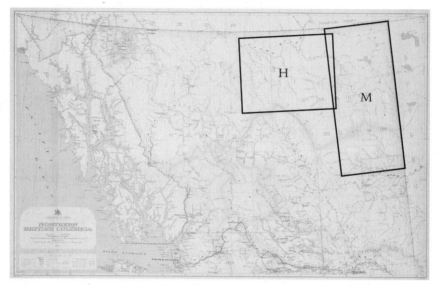

Northern British Columbia in 1917, showing the territories explored and
surveyed by Milligan (M) and Hart (H) in 1913 and 1914. Hart's territory is
expanded below and Milligan's on the facing page. Compare them with the maps
drawn by Milligan on pages 178–79 and Hart on pages 182–83. BCA CM/C28.

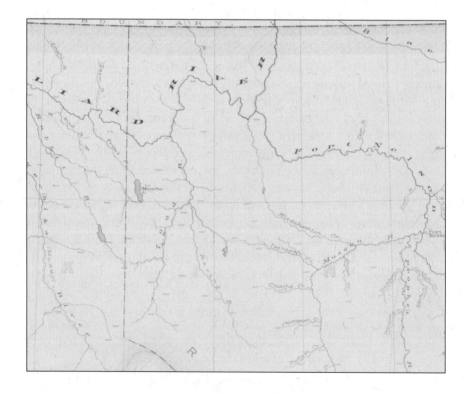

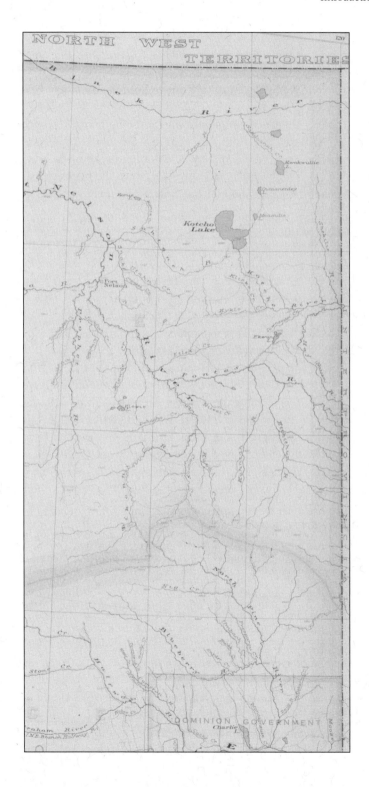

using triangulation Swannell was able to produce an accurate, detailed map that covered a large area. In northwestern BC, Thomas H. Taylor (PLS #51) conducted surveys related to the Groundhog coal leases. In 1911 the federal government completed a survey of the boundaries of the Peace River Block, a large area in the vicinity of Fort St John that it received from the BC government as part of compensation for the construction of the Canadian Pacific Railway. The following year the provincial government hired two surveyors, George Milligan (BCLS #41) from Victoria and John R. Graham (BCLS #70), to do lot surveys adjacent to the western boundary of the Peace River Block in the Halfway and Graham river valleys northwest of Fort St John.

The success of the 1912 surveys prompted the BC government to extend its work even further north in 1913. It hired Swannell to expand his triangulation survey into the Omineca Mountains, instructed Taylor to continue his work in the Groundhog area, hired D.O. Wing (BCLS #76) to survey an area adjacent to Taylor's survey and requisitioned the two explorations of northeastern BC that are the subject of this book.

A bulletin titled "New British Columbia", published by the Legislative Assembly in 1912, estimated that over half of the arable land in the province was located in the Peace River district. The bulletin also noted that "all present knowledge is confined to the valley of the Peace River and its tributaries", while the remainder of the district was little known and the far north was "terra incognita". There were no settlements north of Fort St John in northeastern BC, only one Hudson's Bay post at Fort Nelson. Very few non-native people lived in the area or travelled through it, though in 1898 a small number of Klondikers attempting the overland route from Edmonton to the Yukon passed through the Hay River area to Fort Nelson and northwest to the Liard River. Up to 1913, there had been no detailed government exploration of the area, though two federal surveyors had visited parts of it: R.G. McConnell of the Dominion Geological Survey had explored the Liard River valley in 1887, and William Ogilvie, a Dominion land surveyor, had made a quick survey in 1891 while travelling from the Liard River to Fort St John.

Three First Nations have traditional territories in northeastern BC: the Dunne-za (formerly called Beaver) in the Fort St John area and east to Alberta; the Sekani (Sikanni) west of the Rocky Mountains, but with a small contingent residing between Fort Nelson and the mountains; and the Dene-thah (formerly called Slave or Slavey) in the extreme northeast around Fort Nelson. These First Nations are signatories of Treaty 8, the first numbered treaty to include land in British Columbia. Treaty 8 began in 1899. The Dunne-za signed in 1900, the Dene-thah in 1910 and the Sekani in 1911. The 1912 federal Indian Agent's census report for the Fort Nelson

George Milligan at the end of his 1914 exploration. Frank Swannell photograph; BCA I-58158.

area listed 102 Dunne-za, 129 Dene-thah and 98 Sekani. None lived on a reserve, but followed their traditional lifestyle of hunting and trapping while living in tipis. The Dunne-za had horses. The Sekani and Dene-thah travelled on foot in the summer and used dogsleds in the winter. The Indian Agent described all three groups as temperate and moral.

The provincial government was eager to have an extensive survey of northeastern BC that would produce an accurate, detailed map and provide an assessment of the economic potential of the area (agricultural, mining, forestry, etc.). For the main survey, BC's surveyor general selected George Milligan, a young, talented BC land surveyor who had already spent two years working in the Peace River area. Milligan was to cover the land north of the Peace River Block to at least Fort Nelson, and hopefully to the northern boundary of the province. He would be accompanied by William Cartwright, an agriculturalist who had worked on survey crews for a few years.

At the instructions of the surveyor general, Milligan kept a detailed diary and took photographs of the land and the few people who lived there. His diary is clearly written with the intention of giving the surveyor general in Victoria a sense of being out in the field with him. Almost a century later Milligan's descriptions of the land and people of northeastern BC convey the reader back to that time and give a feeling of being involved in his adventures. His diary records his surveying work and experiences while travelling through rugged remote country. Milligan spent considerable time, particularly in 1914, with the indigenous people of the area, and he provides the earliest written accounts and pictures of their way of life and how they have survived in a harsh land.

The second exploration, led by E.B. Hart, was to cover the northern part of BC from the Rocky Mountains to Fort Nelson, and from 57° north latitude to the northern boundary of BC. Hart, a Boer War veteran, former Hudson's Bay Company employee, mining speculator and self-styled explorer, had produced a report of the area between Dease Lake and the Kechika River (just west of the Rocky Mountains) for the BC government in 1912. He worked on his own to the west of Milligan's area, although he hired First Nations guides and canoemen as necessary. Hart's detailed letters to the surveyor general chronicle the hardships of travelling through this remote region and the difficult life of the few inhabitants of the area. Hart became embroiled in several controversies and the surveyor general had to spend considerable time dealing with these.

The Milligan and Hart explorations provided the first comprehensive information on British Columbia's least-known region. They gathered geographical information, described the economic potential of the land, recorded extensive meteorological data and reported on the way of life of the First Nations in the area. Their surveys resulted in the first detailed maps of the northeastern part of the province, and both Milligan and Hart preserved the First Nations geographical names for the area they covered.

But by the time both men returned to Victoria in November 1914, the BC government, like many others in the world, had turned its attention toward the events of World War I. Milligan and Hart completed their reports and then enlisted in the military. The information collected in these two extensive explorations was filed away and forgotten in the shadow of the Great War.

In the Beginning

G.B. Milligan

George Berry Milligan was born in Victoria on July 9, 1888, the second child of Thomas and Sarah Milligan. Thomas Stamper Milligan had immigrated to Victoria from England as a young man. He worked initially as a real-estate agent and later opened his own accounting firm. Sarah had come from Scotland as a teenager.

Tall and athletic, George was popular with his peers in Victoria. He played rugby for the James Bay Athletic Club and was a member of the 1909–10 Victoria rep team that won both the BC and Pacific Coast championships and played an exhibition game against the New Zealand All Blacks. George decided to become a surveyor at a young age, beginning his apprenticeship with J.H. Gray in 1905 at the age of 16. His older brother, John, also apprenticed to be a surveyor with Gray, starting later in the same year. Gray was a veteran surveyor who had done some of the original Canadian Pacific Railway surveying in BC in the 1870s and later was an engineer on the construction of the rail line. Now in his fifties, he needed help to maintain his busy practice. When the Grand Trunk Pacific Railway started construction through the central interior, Gray received both government and private contracts to survey land in the vicinity of the railroad. Through this work George and John Milligan started their surveying in the interior of the province. (Gray's first work in BC's central interior had been a series of township surveys in the Nechako River valley, followed by a few years in the Bulkley and Skeena river valleys.) George became BCLS #41 in 1910, when he was 21, the youngest possible age to receive a commission, and John BCLS #42 in the same year. Both men then became partners with Gray, forming Gray and Milligan Brothers Surveying.

Dog teams on the Peace River, probably at the end of the 1911 survey season. CVA 65778. (Milligan had a camera that could produce panoramic photographs. This is the first of several in this book, each spread over two pages.)

In 1911, while J.H. Gray and John Milligan continued surveying in the interior, George went to the Peace River area for the first time with a survey crew. He travelled by train, stagecoach and boat to Giscome Portage on the Fraser River above present day Prince George. From there, he and his crew portaged their goods to Summit Lake on the headwaters of the Crooked River, at the beginning of the Arctic drainage. He bought two river boats there and hired two First Nations men as guides. Milligan's crew had to do all the paddling, and at McLeod Lake the guides refused to go any further. Milligan and his crew continued on, but they didn't know the country and met no one on the waterways to help them. Don MacDonald, one of Milligan's crew members, described the journey: "We went on down

First Nations men canoeing on the Skeena River, probably in 1910, when Milligan was surveying in the area along the route of the Grand Trunk Pacific Railway. CVA 65777.

the Pack and Parsnip by ourselves with much trouble since none of us were river men and no one knew which channel to take. At last we came to Finlay Forks and passed to Finlay Rapids where we nearly were swamped."

The first main camp for Milligan and his crew was a few kilometres above Rocky Mountain Portage.

> Many framed abandoned tipis stood here and the cook immediately made use of them for firewood. Soon two Indians came along and were very angry at 'white man for chopping down Indian houses'. They even fired their rifles up river, but peace was restored when someone asked them if they were hungry. They ate and went after we promised not to chop any more Indian houses. Later we found out that one of them was the big chief of the Beavers [Dunne-za], John Chunaman, and the other was Dokie [later chief of the West Moberley band].

Macdonald also remembered what happened later in the season when Milligan's crew moved camp to Hudson's Hope. "A man named Wilson undertook to pack our equipment across the 14-mile portage to Hudson Hope but he dropped much of our gear and we had to return for it ourselves. We let one boat go through the canyon hoping to pick it up below but all we picked up were splinters."

At the same time Gray sent some men with a pack train of horses (initially used during his surveying in the Nechako valley in 1908) through the Pine Pass to the Chetwynd area. On May 26 Frank Beatton, the Hudson's Bay Company factor at Fort St John, noted in his diary: "Three men arrived from Mr Milligan's survey camp south up the Pine River." During the next

"Prairie chickens are plentiful." Milligan's 1912 survey crew living off the land.
LTSA file 3418.

three years Beatton's journals would contain several references to Milligan
and his crew.

Initially Milligan surveyed some coal claims for Neil Gething in the
Rocky Mountain Canyon area near Hudson's Hope. Then the crew went
to nearby Beryl Prairie to pick up the pack train of horses. From there
Milligan travelled south to the Chetwynd area. During the summer and
fall he surveyed a large section of private land along the south boundary of
the Peace River Block and then past the southwest corner. By the time he
completed his surveying in December he must have known that he would
be doing more work in the area in 1912. He left the horses to spend the
winter near Hudson's Hope and six of his men to winter in Fort St John.

Milligan returned to Victoria via Edmonton where he completed the
office work for his surveys and prepared for the upcoming field season. In
1912 Milligan started working on contract for the BC government. Now
that the federal government had completed their survey of the Peace River
Block and marked the boundary of this land, the provincial government
was eager to begin surveying on their land adjoining the block's western
boundary. Both Milligan and J.R. Graham received contracts to survey a
large section of land in the Halfway and Graham river valleys into agricultural lots. Milligan worked mainly in the Halfway River valley. In early
April he left Victoria, and on the 24th Frank Beatton wrote in his diary:
"G.B. Milligan and party arrived with a pack train from LS [Lesser Slave]
Lake." After obtaining the necessary supplies and equipment Milligan and

his crew departed on April 26 for Hudson's Hope to pick up their horses before proceeding to the Halfway River valley to begin surveying.

Milligan divided his large survey crew into two parties. The surveying proceeded smoothly and uneventfully with occasional trips to the Hudson's Bay posts at Fort St John or Hudson's Hope for supplies. By mid October Milligan had completed his contract. He must have anticipated returning to survey in the region in 1913, for once again he left the horses to winter in the Hudson's Hope area. Milligan returned to Victoria to complete the office work from his extensive survey. Soon he would be preparing for an even larger project with the BC government.

E.B. Hart

Ethelbert Hart was baptized in Middlesex, England, on April 28, 1872. As an adult he changed his name to Edward Burton Hart, but he was always known as E.B. Hart. The 1881 and 1891 censuses list his birthplace as Middlesex, but in the 1901 and 1911 Canadian censuses, Hart claims that he was born in Ireland. In some documents, he said that he was born in 1871 and in others 1872. Ethelbert was the fourth child and third son of John and Sarah Hart. John had joined the British army when he was 15 years old and served for almost 22 years. Most of his time was spent overseas, including two years in Canada. Although John had retired from the army with a pension by the time Ethelbert was born, he continued to serve as a volunteer drill instructor and the family lived at the armoury when Ethelbert was young.

Ethelbert's oldest brother, William, became a clerk in a law firm and eventually a solicitor. The second brother, Alfred, was a civil servant. It appeared that Ethelbert was going to follow a similar career path when he received an appointment in the British Postal Service in December 1888, but the 1891 census states that he was working in a savings bank.

John Hart died in 1889, leaving an estate of almost £2000 to his family. Perhaps E.B. inherited his father's adventuresome spirit, and with his two oldest brothers working, he was able to use some of the family inheritance to emigrate to Canada. Hart claimed that he came to Canada in 1889 or 1890, but his presence in the 1891 British census suggests that he must have arrived shortly after that.

The first record for Hart in Canada is in June 1896 when he and Alastair Irvine Robertson filed a pre-emption for 130 hectares along Ta Ta Creek five kilometres from the Kootenay River. (Robertson later became BCLS #24 and worked for a while with Frank Swannell.) The 1898 voter's list shows Hart as a farmer in the Fort Steele area, and in the 1900 list he is a farmer further north in the Windermere region. But Hart and Robertson appeared to do little to improve their land, and in 1900 another person applied to the government to cancel their pre-emption because they did not complete the necessary requirements. The government agent noted that the land had not been occupied for the last 18 months and that the only improvements made were a small log cabin, an unfinished stable and a short piece of drainage ditch. Hart wrote a letter to the gold commissioner in Fort Steele offering an explanation: "my partner A.I. Robertson is now in South Africa serving with the Second Canadian Contingent and I had understood that the government promised in such cases to hold the pre-emption until one year after the close of the war. I am sorry to say that though I am very anxious to hold the pre-emption until next fall when I should be in a position to occupy it, yet it is impossible for me to live there at the present time." The government cancelled Hart and Robertson's pre-emption.

The 1901 census listed Hart as a miner living in Peterborough (now Wilmer), near Invermere. In the late fall that year the *Fort Steele Prospector* reported that the Canadian government was recruiting soldiers for the "Third Canadian Contingent" in the South African War. It said that Ethelbert Hart was one of nine men selected from 49 applicants. He gave his occupation as packer and declared that he was a good rider and a good shot. Likely the military career of John Hart was an important factor for his son's acceptance into the Second Canadian Mounted Rifles. Hart and his fellow recruits left for eastern Canada almost immediately and sailed from Halifax in January 1902. After some training, the Second Canadian Mounted Rifles were sent into action on March 19. They served until the end of May, when the war ended, and during that time were involved in several engagements, including the Battle of Harts River (Boschbult), where the Canadian troops suffered their second highest number of casualties in a single day during that war. At the end of June the Second Canadian Mounted Rifles sailed from South Africa for Halifax, Ethelbert Hart among them.

Hart did not return to the Kootenays after serving in the war. His service medals were sent to Blaine, Washington, in September 1904, and border-crossing records show that he returned to BC in November 1905, arriving in Victoria from Seattle with a group of miners. Soon after, he found work at the Berry Creek Mine near Dease Lake in northwestern BC, operated by Warburton Pike. Hart had been a miner when he lived in the Kootenays and the opportunity to go to Cassiar probably appealed to his sense of adventure. When the mine closed in 1907 due to financial difficulties, Hart decided to remain in the Dease Lake area, so he began searching for other employment.

In the spring of 1908 the Hudson's Bay Company required a manager for their post at Dease Lake. It was a small post, but served a vital role in the HBC's transportation network in the Cassiar region of northwestern

Warburton Pike (right) and Lord Osbourne Beauclerk, partners at the Berry Creek Mine in 1911. Photographer unknown; BCA D-02229.

Warburton Pike

Warburton Pike (1861–1915) was a British adventurer and author who spent many years travelling through the wilderness of northern Canada. In 1897, at the beginning of the Klondike gold rush, Pike became involved with a plan to construct a railway in the Dease Lake area of northwestern BC. In 1902 he invested in and became managing director of the Berry Creek Hydraulic Mining Company. The mine was located on Thibert Creek, near Dease Lake, the main gold-mining area in the Cassiar district at that time. Pike had difficulty recruiting labour due to the mine's remote location. He had property on Saturna Island, one of the Gulf Islands, and lived there when he was not at the mine. He probably met E.B. Hart at Victoria.

The Berry Creek Mine ceased operation in 1907 but reopened a few years later. Pike remained involved with it until the beginning of World War I, when he returned to Britain and attempted to enlist in the army. By then he was 54 years old and, despite his fitness, he was rejected by the military. Despondent at being unable to serve in the war, Pike committed suicide shortly afterwards. Mount Warburton Pike, on Saturna Island, is named for him.

Lake House, the Hudson's Bay Company post at the head of Dease Lake at the end of the trail from Telegraph Creek, 1911. A pack train has arrived with supplies from Telegraph Creek. Marshall Bond photograph; BCA D-02263.

BC. Boats would bring goods up the Stikine River to Telegraph Creek, the HBC's main post in the Cassiar district. From there they were shipped by pack train to Dease Lake, the beginning of the Arctic watershed, where an HBC barge carried goods up and down the 30-kilometre lake. From the outlet of the lake, canoes and other water craft would travel down the Dease River to the Liard, then down the Liard to Fort Simpson on the Mackenzie River. The HBC maintained a series of posts along the waterway.

On June 3 Louis Dixon, the factor at Telegraph Creek, sent a telegram to James Thomson, the head of the HBC in British Columbia:

> I wired you May 21st stating that a new man must be had for Dease and suggesting that Mr Creyke be given the appointment....The Post needs a worker as Mr Arnett [a former HBC employee who operated a trading post on the lake] is gradually capturing the business, and I think Mr Creyke should more than hold his own. Should you not deem it advisable to adopt this suggestion, Mr E.B. Hart who worked for the Berry Creek Mining Co. is looking for a position.

Walter Creyke had been involved in a financial scandal at the HBC post at Telegraph Creek, so Thomson instructed Dixon not to rehire him. Hart had no experience in trapping or operating a trade store, but he was in the area and wanted a job. Thomson wrote to Dixon: "He is not as well suited

Hudson's Bay Company barge at Dease Lake, 1911. Marshall Bond photograph; BCA D-02261.

to the management of the post as I would have liked, but under present circumstances there appears to be no other alternative." In June 1908 the HBC hired Hart to be the post factor at Dease Lake, but instead of making him a permanent employee he was engaged on a monthly salary for one year.

The Hudson's Bay Company's troubles with Hart started almost immediately. On August 12 Dixon sent a confidential letter to Thomson.

> During the past week several parties including Troxel, in charge of Hyland's train, G.D. Cox and Jimmy Porter, have brought out from Dease reports of scandalous conduct on the part of Mr Hart.
>
> It is alleged that he has attempted unnatural practices with several small boys, including W.S. Simpson's [Walter Scott Simpson, later Indian Agent for the region] second son who is at the lake. The pack train has just arrived and on asking Mr Day about the matter he tells me it is common talk in there.
>
> Whether this charge is true or not, and I fear from all reports it is, it is evident that a man with charges such as this being spread against him cannot remain in charge of a company post.
>
> Should you deem action necessary before your arrival, kindly telegraph me your instructions.

James Thomson was about to make his annual visit to the company posts in the Cassiar region. He faced a dilemma. If the charges were true he needed to act quickly. After the company's recent difficulties with Walter

Creyke regarding misappropriation of money, they did not want another scandal in the district. At the same time, Hart's legal rights needed to be protected, and the charges against him had to be proved. The HBC also needed a person for the Dease Lake post and no one else was available. Thomson's report to his superiors in Winnipeg no longer exists, but he must have been satisfied that Hart could remain. In the meantime, James Porter, the gold commissioner and government agent at Telegraph Creek, began to investigate the charges while Thomson searched for a replacement.

In January 1909, with the situation still unresolved, Hart travelled to Telegraph Creek. On February 3 Dixon sent a telegram to Thomson:

> On January 26th I wired you in code: Hart here. Has requested Indian Agent take action on reports last summer. Admits speaking to Indians but declines action…. In justice I have obtained agents promise action when Indians return or obtain apology. Is this satisfactory to you. Hart working well.
>
> In reply I was informed of your absence and on the following morning I sent Hart back to the Post.
>
> I cannot find by the code that the spreading of reports without publication affords grounds for an action.

William Ware became the new factor at Telegraph Creek in April 1909. In his instructions to Ware, Thomson wrote:

> I communicated to you the report of an alleged misdemeanour by E.B. Hart. I do not know what action if any has been taken by the authorities or himself. He informed me he would retire from the service in any event…. You will acquaint yourself of conditions on your arrival and the Provincial Government Agent, Mr Porter, will be pleased to give you all information.

On May 22 Ware wrote to Thomson:

> I think that affair in which Mr Hart's name was connected seems to have dropped. I understood that he was here during the winter and appeared to be on visiting terms with the Porters. I gather that his intent is to stay on…. I have not met Mr Porter but will make a point of doing so tomorrow and will write or wire you further on the subject.

On May 31 Ware sent a telegram to Thomson informing him that the authorities were not prosecuting Hart, but Porter's opinion on the subject was still undecided. He also reported that, on May 30, he had received a letter from Hart addressed to the previous factor, Dixon, tendering his resignation. One of the reasons cited in his resignation was Dixon's apparent support of Arnett, the operator of the other store on Dease Lake, in a controversy regarding prices being charged. Ware told Thomson that he was writing Hart that his resignation was being forwarded to Thomson for consideration.

In a reply on June 11 Thomson wrote:

> It may be as well to state to you frankly that I do not know of any other
> man available. I am not anxious that Mr Hart should remain but in view
> of the developments which have taken place since his letter of resignation
> was sent in, he might possibly remain for the present. I would therefore
> ask you to be good enough to write him to this effect. It is desirable to
> the Company's interests particularly in respect of the transport service
> for McDames Creek and Liard that Dease Lake Post be maintained but
> of course if a suitable Post manager cannot be secured, there will be no
> alternative to close it, temporarily at least.

On June 15 Ware wrote a detailed letter to Thomson regarding Hart.

> I visited Mr Porter with the object of discussing with him Mr Hart's af-
> fair. I learnt that the case was not being taken up against Hart but that he
> came in to Telegraph Creek this spring to have the matter investigated.
> Nothing was done as there were no witnesses around at the time.
>
> Mr Porter stated to me that he did not know what to think about the
> affair, but he was inclined to believe that possibly no crime was commit-
> ted but blames Hart for being extremely familiar with the Indian youths
> and that he has only himself to blame for bringing about the scandal.

Ware also commented on Hart's resignation letter, noting:

> He defends his actions in controversy with Arnett over prices charged for
> supplies to the latter and other matters more or less of a personal nature.
> It appears that Mr Dixon had decided some point in Arnett's favour,
> which caused Hart to close his letter with the following remarks: "I have
> only this to add. Your letter to me, in which you accuse me of an untruth
> and also of sharp practise leaves only one course open to me. I beg you
> therefore to accept my resignation from my position with the Hudson's
> Bay Co."

Ware told Thomson:

> From private source I do not think that Hart is desirous of leaving the
> service and consider it wise to let him be in suspense as to whether his
> resignation will be accepted or not, especially as it would be very inconve-
> nient for him to leave until you had another man in sight to fill his place.

In late June Hart wrote to Ware: "I have no wish at all to leave the company's service and am quite willing to withdraw my resignation. My sole
reason for resigning is that it appeared the only course open to me under
the circumstances." His 1909 and 1910 evaluations by the company indi-
cated that his work was satisfactory, but he was never offered permanent
employment. He remained factor at the Hudson's Bay post until the fall of
1910, when he went to Victoria for hernia surgery. He returned to Telegraph Creek in May, but it appears he did not go back to Dease Lake. The
1911 census lists Hart with the other HBC employees at Telegraph Creek,

although he declares his occupation as post manager. He worked for the HBC until his departure in mid October.

Hart returned to Telegraph Creek in the spring of 1912, this time as a prospector. He had purchased a free miner's certificate while in Victoria the previous winter and had convinced a group of people in Victoria to sponsor him in staking claims in the Turnagain River area, a tributary of the Kechika River northeast of Dease Lake. Among these people were two prominent lawyers, H.B. Robertson and H.G.L. Heistermann, along with a young lawyer who worked with this firm – Alexander Milligan, George Milligan's youngest brother. Hart was in the field until early October. By the time he left Telegraph Creek on October 16 he had staked five claims.

When Hart returned to Victoria he met British Columbia's surveyor general, George Dawson, and convinced him to pay for a report he wrote based on his knowledge of the Dease Lake area and his 1912 travels along the Turnagain and Kechika rivers. Hart asked for $2000, but Dawson consulted the minister of Lands and then offered him $250, which he accepted. Hart was staying at the Union Club in Victoria, and he heard that Premier Richard McBride had disparaged the value of his report. He wrote to McBride:

> I regret that my report on the Cassiar should have been found to be of so
> little value to the government, and whilst thanking you for your kindness
> and the trouble you have taken on the matter, I beg to state that I should
> prefer to withdraw both report and map rather than accept the offer made
> by the surveyor general's department.

The premier did not reply, but sent Hart's note to Dawson.

Hart applied to the surveyor general for employment as an explorer for the 1913 field season. Dawson turned him down, feeling that Hart would not be able to produce any useful results. Then he received orders to hire Hart for two seasons. Somehow Hart managed to gain the support of Dr Henry Young, MLA for Atlin and northwestern BC. He had lived in Young's riding during his time in northwestern BC and part of the government's surveying exploration would be in his riding. Young was provincial secretary, minister of Education, and one of Premier McBride's most influential cabinet members. He provided Hart with a personal letter of support.

So, in the spring of 1913, Hart was ready to embark on a new adventure as an explorer.

William Cartwright

William Cartwright was born in England in 1881. He took agricultural training there before immigrating to Canada in 1903. He worked as a farmer and on the survey crew of E.P. Colley (PLS #67) for a few years. In December 1911 Cartwright returned to England to visit his family. He was supposed to sail back to Canada with Colley on the *Titanic*, but family members persuaded him to remain longer (Colley perished in the sinking). In 1913 the BC Ministry of Agriculture hired Cartwright as an agriculturalist to accompany George Milligan on his exploration and to help him with the surveying.

William Cartwright in northern BC. William Cartwright family collection.

Spring and Summer 1913

G.B. Milligan

On May 3, 1913, the surveyor general wrote George Milligan a detailed letter of instructions stressing the importance of the expedition.

> As the nature of your work is to a large extent experimental, this being
> the first occasion on which a British Columbia Land Surveyor has been
> sent out for such a length of time, you are to examine a totally unknown
> country and it is my sincere wish that you will be able to make plans and
> reports on this section of the country which will warrant the Government
> in confiding such work to a Land Surveyor....
>
> I wish to impress upon you the fact that all your labour of one and
> a half years, and the expense to which the Department will be put, will
> be represented by your report, and ... it is of vital importance that your
> report be as full and complete as possible.

Dawson also stated that the expedition's two main purposes were to map and record the physical features of the country and to get some idea of its resources. He instructed Milligan to examine "that portion of the Peace River Block lying north of the Dominion Railway Block", especially the eastern section, and not to survey any area west of the Fort Nelson drainage, because that would be covered by E.B. Hart. But he acknowledged that Hart was exploring the area assigned to him alone and without "the facilities for obtaining geographical information that you have", so he encouraged Milligan to look over Hart's area if he had time.

The surveyor general then provided specifics regarding the surveying and mapping.

> You will be expected to furnish this Department with information as to
> the topographical features of this District and to prepare sketches which
> will show the main physical features and which will be of sufficient

accuracy as to be useful for mapping purposes and which, together with your description, will enable a subsequent explorer to recognize that section of the country from the physical features found by him. In connection with this part of the work, you will be expected to use your knowledge as a surveyor and determine, as accurately as possible that latitude and approximate longitude of as many points as is deemed necessary. This portion of the work in which you will doubtless take a professional interest, requires little comment from me.

You will appreciate, that to make this trip a success it will be necessary to make rough triangulations of portions of the country and track surveys over others and to keep up plotting in the field so that you may have a record on which to show the country and also notes as to its character.

Regarding the resources of the area:

Note the existence and extent of any land suitable for settlement of any character. You will examine carefully and report on the river valleys travelled by you and will estimate the extent of flat or bench land found on the same, together with the possibilities of both or either being used for settlement.

[Report on] the natural resources of the country and the possibilities of agriculture or cattle raising, also the quality and quantity of timber and any signs of minerals, and the existence of water powers…. [And be] particularly careful to look for any evidence of petroleum as reports are current that oil has been found in this District….

As this District is unknown country all information gathered by you will be of interest.

The government had reserved this area from agricultural and industrial development until it received Milligan's report.

Dawson told Milligan to "keep a full and voluminous diary" and make notes on the country every day, to take as many photographs as possible, to make daily barometer readings to help establish elevations where he was working and to record temperatures each day to "give some idea of the climatic conditions."

He concluded by telling Milligan "to report to me on every possible occasion which presents itself so as to get it into the hands of this Department as soon as practicable as it is possible that there may be a demand on the part of the public for this section."

For a young, talented surveyor like Milligan this expedition provided a unique opportunity. He did not have a full survey crew – only William Cartwright and a packer – and he was going into a fairly flat area that was not suitable for the triangulation surveying that Frank Swannell was doing, so he would have to develop his own surveying techniques. There were almost no surveying stations in the area, so he would have to determine the most effective method of covering this large area and then establish his own surveying network, all while being mostly self-sufficient for a lengthy amount of time. His assignment also involved a great variety of tasks: surveying, mapping, reporting on resources, recording the climate, taking photographs, keeping a detailed diary, managing the logistics of the 18-month expedition, and establishing relationships with Hudson's Bay Company staff and the indigenous people of the area.

A front page article in Victoria's *Daily Colonist* on May 8, 1913, reported on the significance of the Milligan expedition:

Victoria Party to Peace River

Among the survey parties being sent out this season by the surveyor general of the Province the exploration party which starts today for the Peace River district is an entirely new departure and one which is fraught with much importance to the development of the northern portion of British Columbia. [The district] is at present hardly known to all, has been reserved from all alienation and is too far away and difficult of access for any pre-emptions to be taken up for some time. This expedition is a preliminary even to any land surveying, and it is expected, will be the means of securing for the Government information which will greatly assist in the next steps to be taken when the progress of development has begun.

The article noted Milligan's surveying experience and commented that "the expedition is one which will give scope for the employment of a good deal more than the abilities required for the routine of survey work." It also mentioned William Cartwright. "Mr Cartwright has had an agricultural training in England and for ten years has ranched in this country, so that he is well qualified to determine the quality of the various soils encountered and their possibilities, when taken in conjunction with the climatic conditions, for agriculture."

The article concluded by stating "when these gentlemen come out again in the fall of 1914 they should have a tale to tell which will be both of enthralling interest and of the utmost value to those responsible for guiding the destinies of the Province."

Part of Milligan's preparations for his exploration was applying to be a fellow of the Royal Geographical Society in London, England. He had two excellent references: Major C.B. Simonds, a surveyor, and George G. Aitken, chief geographer of the province. His application was accepted in June 1913. (E.B. Hart had applied successfully to be a fellow in the society in 1912; he had also used Major Simonds as one of his references, while the other was J.S.H. Matson, a Victoria newspaperman.)

Milligan and Cartwright left Victoria on May 9, 1913, along with Frank Swannell and his assistant, George Copley, who were headed for the Omineca region in north-central BC. Swannell wrote in his diary: "Milligan, leaving for Peace River, gets great send off from his friends." Swannell would meet again Milligan at Fort St John at the end of the 1914 field season. Milligan and Cartwright travelled by train to Edmonton. While Milligan gathered supplies there Cartwright travelled ahead to make arrangements for transportation. The route to Fort St John via Edmonton was one of four listed in the provincial government's 1912 bulletin entitled "New British Columbia". Milligan had used this route at the end of the 1911 field season and in 1912. It involved rail, steamer and wagon and was the easiest route to northeastern BC when carrying a large amount of equipment. Milligan had heard that the Hudson's Bay Company post at Fort Nelson might be temporarily closed so he purchased most of the supplies that he would need for 18 months at the HBC store in Edmonton.

His diary began on May 23 when he left Edmonton at 9 AM.

> Travel via CNR [Canadian Northern Railway] to Athabasca Landing 94 miles [150 km], arriving at 4:50 PM. Train travels slowly on account of poor road bed being mostly sandy. Meet Cartwright who has arranged for passage and freight, etc. up the Athabasca River. It is reported we will be delayed on Slave Lake as ice has not yet all gone out.

Along the route to Peace River Crossing, the men stop for lunch at Bear Head "where Indians have little moose in captivity". RBCM PN03480.

Steamers on the Peace River. LTSA (panorama).

The next morning the two men left on the steamer *Athabasca*, the first passenger boat of the season. Milligan wrote:

> The boat carries large passenger list and lots of freight. The passengers are mostly people who are returning to their northern homes having spent the winter in civilization. There are also many who are going into Peace River country to take up homesteads. There is an amusing English couple (just out), man and wife. The husband is an old country solicitor and expects to follow his profession at Grouard. When outfitting at Edmonton he asked the H.B. Co. district manager for advice as to the kind of canoe he should take with him.

By the end of the day they were about 8 kilometres from Mirror Landing, the end of their boat trip, when they reached a riffle. "After many futile attempts to get above this riffle we tie up for the night." It took the crew two days "and not till they had unloaded about ten tons freight did they manage to slide the vessel over the shallow water at 9 PM, arriving at Mirror Landing at 10:30 PM." From there, wagon teams took the freight and luggage 30 kilometres to Salteaux Landing, where they boarded another steamer for two days of travel to the head of Lesser Slave Lake.

On June 1 Milligan and Cartwright began a three-day, 130-kilometre wagon trip carrying some of their freight to Peace River Crossing, where the HBC was holding a steamer until they arrived. They waited two days at Peace River Crossing for the rest of the freight to arrive, but on June 6 they received word that it had just been shipped, so they arranged for the supplies (more than 400 kg) to be shipped to Fort St John on another steamer.

One day, while on the steamer to Fort St John: "Moose and calf are sighted by pilot on the right bank of river. After about 5 minutes rifle fire from about ten different rifles the moose is finally mortally wounded when we land and haul the animal on board. It was the intention to catch the calf but as it had been unfortunately hit by stray bullet it was found necessary to despatch."

After more than a month of travel from Victoria, Milligan and Cartwright arrived at Fort St John on June 10. The freight they had on board was stored at the Hudson's Bay Company warehouse, and then they continued upstream for Hudson's Hope, camping at Dog Island. The next morning they left early, "but the wood taken on there was found to be too green for steamer so about two miles above Cache Creek steamer ties up and crew spend three hours cutting dry wood." The high water and strong current made travel slow and they only reached a few kilometres above the Halfway River that day. The next morning they arrived at Hudson's Hope and picked up Milligan's horses that he'd wintered there. On June 13 they returned to Fort St John where they stayed in a spare HBC cabin.

Milligan and Cartwright spent four days at Fort St John getting ready for their field work. For the first three days it rained, and rain would dominate the weather through much of the summer. Milligan noted, "Peace River very high and rising. Continual stream of drift wood floating down and water loaded with sediment." The men were advised to wait a day after the rain stopped: "the creeks to the north would be unfordable and best to delay a day till trail dries on the steep hill."

Fort St John viewed from the bench above the Peace River. LTSA (panorama).

Fur press at Fort St John. LTSA file 3418.

In a letter to the surveyor general, Milligan wrote about a difficulty that he encountered at Fort St John. "We were unable to secure a guide who was familiar with the country north of the Dominion Block, there being no white men that travel these parts and the Beaver Indians [Dunne-za] who hunt in the North Pine country are undependable and are of little use in any capacity." Eventually, Milligan hired Fred Hazen, a local farmer, as packer. When the sun finally came out on June 17, Milligan made observations for the local meridian time to assist his surveying. While at the fort he also took daily barometer readings to try to establish elevation both at the high water of the Peace River and at the top of the plateau above the river. Throughout this exploration he meticulously took daily barometer and temperature readings and recorded the weather. His field work includes a large book of meteorological data.

In the evening of June 18 Milligan, Cartwright and Hazen left Fort St John following the Nelson trail north to Fort Nelson. The first 60 kilometres took them through the federal government's Peace River Block. Cartwright described the route in his government report: "The horse trail from Fort St John north through the Dominion government reserve is well defined, having been much used of late years by the surveyors' pack trains and provides good travelling to the Blueberry River." Milligan noted in his report: "On the plateau north of Fort St John, included within the Peace River Block, are extensive areas of excellent land, and in comparison with the country travelled farther north, no areas were encountered to equal this in desirability from an agricultural point of view."

Blueberry River in the vicinity of the township surveys north of the Peace River Block, where Milligan began his exploratory surveying in 1913. LTSA.

Like many pack trips there were difficulties at first. The next morning the men had "good intention for early start but horses strayed and not till 4:30 [PM] did we get them into camp, too late for start." That evening they "staked out six horses as precaution". The next morning, shortly after starting, "Sam the horse throws his pack and makes back for St John. Although Hazen spends 3 or 4 hours hunting fails to find him." It started raining around 11 AM and continued until 6:30. "Soil more or less clayish and water stays on surface making trail wet." That evening they camped at the Montagneuse Creek crossing. The next morning the men were "delayed ½ hour crossing Montagneuse Creek, 1 horse being stuck in the claying banks." It rained again for much of the day and Milligan noted that it was "very wet and miserable".

On June 22 the three men crossed the north boundary of the Peace River Block into Township 113. This township, along with townships 111 and 115, was part of a small parcel of provincial government land north of the block that had been surveyed by J.R. Graham. After leaving the Peace River Block, Milligan did not meet anyone until September. Although this was Dunne-za territory it was not used often in the summer by the First Nations people, and Milligan would soon learn the reason for this. The heavy rain and poor drainage in the area made travel difficult. To make matters worse, the summer of 1913 was particularly wet, with rainfall on more than half of the days.

The men passed over a summit with 75 metres elevation gain, then followed a small stream down to the Blueberry River. "Recent rains have made the trail very wet, small streams carrying surface water in all directions on each side of summit.... Blueberry River too deep to ford and camp on south side." The next day the men stayed at the same camp while they dried their rigging and packs and made a raft. In the afternoon Milligan crossed the river on Croppy, one of J.H. Gray's Nechako horses that had been brought into the Peace River area in 1911. He followed the trail up the Blueberry River to view some of the country. The crew's dog, Prespa-tou, "swims river and has meal off dead horse – evidently died last winter." On June 24 the weather finally began to clear. The men rafted their supplies across the Blueberry while the horses swam the river, and they camped on the north side.

Milligan spent most of the summer of 1913 in the drainage of the North Pine River (today called the Beatton River), one of the main tributaries on the north side of the Peace, flowing into it downstream from Fort St John. The 240-kilometre-long North Pine is the principal river on the south side of the divide between the watersheds of the Peace and Fort Nelson rivers in the area where Milligan was working. Milligan began surveying in the area immediately north of the Blueberry River, near the north boundary of Township 113. There are three creeks – Buick, Umbach and Prespatou (named for their dog) – that flow southeast in almost parallel drainages into the Blueberry River, which runs almost east into the North Pine. These three drainages are also parallel to the North Pine. Across a low summit to the north of these three creeks, Nig Creek (named for their black horse) flows almost directly east into the North Pine. North of Nig Creek, the North Pine also runs east, parallel to this creek, for several kilometres before turning and flowing southeast.

The Nelson trail, the main route through this area, was primarily used as a winter trail. Milligan wrote: "Until this year the Nelson trail was used by the Treaty Party who annually made the trip from Fort St John to Fort Nelson in connection with the affairs of the Indian Department. They have now abandoned the route, however, and reach Fort Nelson by the Liard and Nelson rivers." Besides the Nelson trail Milligan and his crew found many others used by the Dunne-za (Beaver). Milligan wrote:

> During our first summer in the country we travelled with horses, fol-
> lowing, generally, the Beaver Indian trails. In making one's way across this
> country without a guide, great difficulty is experienced in keeping to the
> right trail, owing to the confusing number of branch trails which run in
> every direction, as a result of the Indians being continually on the move,
> opening up new trails and hunting new ground and following the moose
> about.

He described his surveying methods in a letter to the surveyor general in the fall of 1913:

> I have adopted the method of track survey between points fixed by
> astronomical observations, the latitudes being obtained mostly from
> circum-meridian altitudes of north and south stars and the differences of

longitude on observation of east and west stars for LMT [local meridian time]. I have been using the 5-inch micrometer transit almost entirely, and although I have a sextant I find that I can obtain much more satisfactory results with the transit and shall certainly take it with me wherever it can be carried. The watch used is a "Blockley" – half chronometer and being carefully rated I am confident that the differences of longitude obtained from it are sufficiently accurate for purposes of mapping.

A track survey is a simple method used by many explorers to map an area. The explorer used a compass to obtain a direction. Then he walked at a steady pace in that direction for a certain amount of time. If his average walking speed was 5 kilometres per hour and he walked east for 12 minutes, then he would cover a kilometre in that direction. If he then walked N30°E for 18 minutes he would mark a distance of 1.5 kilometres in that direction on his sketched map. Another track-survey method was to count the number of steps and multiply it by the average distance of the pace.

Although this was a primitive form of mapping, experienced explorers could make a fairly accurate map. To improve the accuracy of his work Milligan made several loops during his surveying. He would start at a location and then return to it via a different route. By calculating and plotting the route he had followed he could see on the map how close he had come to his original starting place. The amount of error would be averaged over the route that he followed. In his track survey Milligan mapped the Nelson and other trails and the numerous creeks of the area that they were following. By recrossing known features (like a definite location on the trail or a creek crossing) from different directions he could average their location on his map, making it even more precise. To fill in the area covered during his surveying Milligan would also sketch the local countryside, noting swamps and other features close to his route.

Milligan's Blockley was a specially made watch (by Herbert Blockley & Company in Great Britain) that could be used as a chronometer. Many explorers around the world at that time, including fellows of the Royal Geographic Society, used a Blockley. Although it was a precise instrument it did not keep totally accurate time. Before going into the field a person would observe the Blockley for several days against an accurate time piece to see how much time it gained or lost. This would be its rating. At the end of the time in the field the instrument would once again be checked to see if the rating remained the same. Any difference would be averaged over the number of days in the field. Milligan had another watch as a back-up in case anything happened to the Blockley, and Cartwright also had a watch. In his final government report Milligan wrote: "In moving our supplies up to the Sikanni, several trips were necessary between the north boundary of the [Peace River] Block and the Sikanni [Chief River]: advantage was taken of this in obtaining watch rating which assisted in carrying fairly accurate difference of longitude along the main line of surveying."

Before going into the field Milligan would also have gone to a place with a known longitude and recorded the time when the sun was at its highest point in the sky. This is called local meridian time (LMT). Since the earth is divided into 360 degrees of longitude and rotates on its axis every 24 hours, every degree of longitude is four minutes. By calculating the difference in time from the known longitude one could calculate the longitude at their location. Because longitude lines converge from the equator toward the poles it was also important to establish latitude at the point of observation so that the distance of a degree of longitude could be calculated for mapping.

Along his route, Milligan would record the local meridian time at a station either by taking a survey measurement on the sun or the stars. During the day, he usually measured LMT when the sun was at its zenith. But he could also measure the sun's position at certain other times of the day and calculate LMT using an almanac of solar data that he carried with him. On clear nights he would often use stars to make survey measurements. There are more than 50 stars that he could use, but Milligan made his observations on a handful that he knew, including Polaris. In addition to LMT he could take survey measurements (also called star shots) and use data from a nautical almanac to establish latitude and longitude at important locations during his exploration. He would then compare the calculations from his track survey with the observations. By taking latitudes and longitudes throughout his expedition Milligan could further improve the accuracy of his track surveys. In 1913 he used a transit to make his sun and star observations as precise as possible.

On June 25 Milligan began his survey while travelling up Buick Creek, the most westerly of the three parallel drainages flowing into the Blueberry River. He wrote in his journal: "Made track survey (pocket compass and distance timed) of trail from Blueberry to camp Buick Creek." He noted: "Have trouble at crossing of Buick Creek, water overflowing bank. Trail very wet from recent rains." He continued his track survey the next day as the crew followed the trail across a low divide to the east to Umbach Creek, which they reached in the early afternoon. "Umbach Creek is impossible to ford at present stage being about 12 feet [3.5 m] deep and 50 feet [15 m] wide." Once again the men had to build a raft and swim the horses, which took until early evening. The next morning Milligan made a cross section of the Umbach valley by surveying from the creek across the valley to the hills above it, again using his pocket compass and Blockley. The cross section was done at about a 90 degree angle to the direction of the trail. Milligan used this cross section to measure the width and direction of the valley and examine terrain away from the trail. The surveying that Milligan did during

Tipi poles remain in a Dunne-za camping area on the flats of the North Pine River. LTSA (panorama).

the first days of his exploration became the pattern for his work during the summer of 1913.

The crew continued heading north through what Milligan described as "uninteresting country." They passed through sections of muskeg and had to build bridges across several narrow creeks that were deep after the recent rains. Milligan noted that the mosquitoes were bad. On June 29, "after descending down a gradual slope for 4 miles [6.5 km] we came to Nig Creek which was easily forded.... After crossing Nig Creek we continue northerly and enter into a muskeg country travelling up a small creek to its summit in the swamps." By mid afternoon the men stopped to camp because the horses were "fairly well done on account [of] coming through the muskeg."

On the last day of June, they reached the North Pine River.

> After leaving camp this morning [and] travelling east of north we descended rapidly from the upper muskeg bench at the foot of which we came out of the timber on to the bank of a clear lake which although only 6 chains [120 m] wide was about ½ mile [800 m] long. The trail follows closely along the west shore and after leaving the lake turns to the NE through Indian camping ground in some meadows and then a few hundred feet further on through timber. Much to our surprise and relief we are on the banks of the North Pine River. The river is muddy and at this point about 6 chains wide and upon fording with a horse was found to be about 2 to 4 feet [~1 m] deep. We make camp on the open flats.

Milligan also remarked that "the Indians evidently winter their horses here as their winter quarters were found amongst the timber."

Milligan, Cartwright and Hazen spent three days at the North Pine. The weather turned rainy again. The crew built a cache to store some of their supplies while they surveyed around the area, and Milligan did some of his office work. On the third day there was sufficient sun for Milligan to make an observation for local meridian time.

On July 4 Hazen and Cartwright packed the horses back south to Nig Creek while Milligan continued his track survey by making a loop around the area. "The country passed through is entirely a muskeg country with the exception of two low pine ridges running down at right angles to my course. The timber in the muskeg is a scrubby spruce and tamarac. The moss is about 1-3 feet [30–90 cm] deep and in places very wet and soft." The sky was clear that night at Nig Creek so he "observed stars till 2 AM for circum-meridian altitudes. Daylight at 2 and very cold." During the following day the men remained at camp while Milligan observed the altitude of the sun for local meridian time and calculated the amount of error in his watch time as he had done at Fort St John.

From Nig Creek the crew returned to Umbach Creek along the "Tredwell new trail east of muskegs – very fair." Milligan surveyed the trail using his compass and Blockley. On July 7 he wrote in his diary. "The rain of the last two days has flooded all the creeks and sloughs, Umbach Creek

Milligan's crew on the Nelson trail, crossing open flats along the North Pine River. LTSA.

having risen 5 feet [1.5 m] during the night – delayed about 3 hours build-ing bridge across flooded creek near camp and finally get all horses and outfit across at 7:30. Start out for Umbach Creek crossing arriving 10:30 PM." The following day the sun reappeared. "Umbach Creek overflowing its banks is now about 25 feet [7.5 m] deep and rising and 100 ft [30 m] wide. Making raft." In the late afternoon "with considerable difficulty move outfit and horses across Umbach Creek. Take PM sun observations and two stars in the evening for latitude." As the crew travelled back to Buick Creek, Milligan noted that the trail was "very wet, muskeg and soft."

By July 9 the three men had returned to the Blueberry where they found the river still too high to ford. Milligan took an observation of the sun for local meridian time. The next day the crew built a raft with trees they had to haul by horse from almost two kilometres away. They crossed the Blue-berry in the afternoon. Milligan's first trip through the North Pine drainage would become the pattern for his surveying during the summer of 1913: a track survey with loops; observations on the sun and stars to establish lati-tude and longitude at several locations and provide a check on the accuracy of his track survey; making notes of the geography of the area; and record-ing evidence of the First Peoples' use of the land.

The following day Hazen and Cartwright returned to Fort St John for the rest of the supplies that they had left there. While they were gone Mil-ligan spent time "calculating and checking astronomical observations taken on trip to Pine" and did "office work on plans, etc."

The North Pine River valley. Milligan found that the viewpoints along this river were not adequate for a triangulation survey of this river. LTSA.

On July 15 Milligan left camp and "took Aiken's trail towards the Pine River. Pack on back and dog carrying 30 lbs [13 kg]. My idea on making this trip was to look at the country generally and to determine whether the trough of the Pine would be useful in any way in carrying a system of triangles northward up the valley." Milligan wanted to see if the banks of the river valley had sufficiently open, high slopes to make a triangulation survey through this major drainage. A triangulation survey would be more accurate and enable Milligan to cover more territory. Unfortunately the topography of the North Pine valley did not facilitate this type of survey.

Milligan noted: "The trail travelled today is blocked in many places by fallen timber and rains of the last few days has left considerable surface water." This area, part of townships 113 and 115, had already been surveyed into one-mile sections; by recording his time Milligan could determine his rate of travel and check the accuracy of his track survey. He camped on top of a hill above the Pine River that night and returned to his main camp the following evening.

On July 18, a week after leaving, Cartwright and Hazen returned. The next day they packed for another trip to the North Pine crossing and made a cache of supplies to be left at Blueberry. The river was now low enough to ford with horses. "Leave the ford at 7 PM and move along Nelson Trail to Buick Ck Crossing. Arrive camp dark, bad mud holes along trail. 2 or 3 horses down and packs wetted. Mosquitoes bad." When they arrived at Umbach Creek they found that the creek had dropped three metres but was still too deep to ford and they had to build a raft again to cross it.

A small lake in the North Pine area. Milligan travelled through a lot of muskeg or marshy areas like this. LTSA (panorama).

Milligan wanted to take time to explore and survey the Nig Creek drainage. On July 22 he left camp in the morning with Croppy the horse carrying instruments and enough supplies for three days. He camped that night at Nig Creek.

> Leave Croppy on picket and strike out after breakfast a little to east of north. About a mile from the creek I came across Indian trail threading its way through brushy swamp with a general direction of NE. This I followed for about 2 miles on same course when the trail swings abruptly through pine and poplar to SE and in about half a mile found myself at an Indian camping ground beautifully situated in an opening amongst the poplars on the bank of Nig Creek.

Milligan followed the trail downstream for a short distance before returning to camp. The pack train arrived around 4 PM. "Thunder commences about 2:30 followed at 4:30 with heavy rains and hail (big as grouse eggs). Storm ends with wind from north followed by calm and sky clearing."

Instead of going directly north to the North Pine River as they had done before, Milligan, Cartwright and Hazen travelled up Nig Creek for about 20 kilometres where they located a trail heading north. They followed this trail over a low wet summit through mostly burnt pine country down to the North Pine. The men camped on the south bank of the river, but Milligan crossed it on Croppy to locate the Nelson trail on the north side.

The next day Hazen left with nine horses for Fort St John to pick up more supplies before the men headed north. While he was gone Milligan

and Cartwright constructed a second cache on the North Pine. "We have so far been very particular about caches, building them on top of tree stumps cut off about 15 ft [4.5 m] above the ground and covered by tent. The stumps are peeled of bark and tin nailed on where available. The surrounding trees are also cut down so that squirrels can't jump from them." Milligan observed that "judging by marks on the trees on the flat the river this spring has been at great height. There is a deposit of new silt on the lower flats 10 ft [3 m] above present stage in places knee deep."

After completing the cache the two men forded the North Pine, reached the Nelson trail about 800 metres north and headed downstream. Milligan described how the trail "followed for the most part along the bench on the north side of the Pine River and in places goes some distance back from the river presumably to obtain better crossings of the numerous creek gulches, some of which are 1 or 2 hundred feet [30–60 m] deep." He noted some small, open flats along the river. "With exception of these flats and a small proportion of the country which has been fire swept spruce muskegs was noticeably predominant in every direction." Along the way "our kitchen mare strayed off the trail this PM at an inappropriate moment and Carty returns to hunt for her, while I keep on with the other three horses, ford the Pine at the lower crossing and camp at our camp made July 1, and up to time of entering through 9 PM Carty has not returned."

Cartwright arrived the next morning with the mare and the two men travelled south to Nig Creek. Milligan had now surveyed a loop that covered

Open flats along the Blueberry River. Milligan believed that this area had the best agricultural land in the region he explored. LTSA (panorama).

Nig Creek and the North Pine. While they were at this camp Milligan made an observation on the sun. He had previously made an observation at this location, so by recording the time he could measure the error in his watches during the interval. On August 1 he hiked down Nig Creek and followed a First Nations trail to the North Pine River. He crossed to the opposite bank and hiked about three kilometres downriver, where he found what appeared to be a well-used trail heading northward away from the river.

> The country passed through was primarily spruce, poplar and jack pine, soil thin and clayish. From openings along the high bench of the Pine I could get views along the Pine valley and as far as I could see, everywhere the timber growth was the same pine, poplar and spruce. On the lower flat in the bends of the river there are good patches of spruce timber. Everywhere the ground is wet and cold – only on the exposed poplar ridges is there any vegetation (grass, pea vine), the remainder being wet, clayish soil, moss-covered and in places boggy.

When he returned to the ford, he headed upriver.

> About ½ mile up I noticed Indian tipi poles on opposite side of river on top of bench or bluff. I might here mention that this cut of crumbling sandstone was the first rock in place noticed on this trip. Huge blocks of sandstone had broken off and fallen crumbling into the river. Generally speaking the bank of the Pine [is] composed of alluvial till and in places bluish clay and mud. Upon fording the river I found the Indians' last winter's camp on a trail going northerly up river.

On August 2 Milligan and Cartwright followed a trail that headed south over a low ridge and down into Prespatou Creek. This drainage is between Umbach Creek to the west and the North Pine River to the east. From his campsite that evening Milligan wrote: "Looking across to the south and west from across our camp there is what appears to be a sea of spruce muskegs stretching away to the foot of a low rise, probably a mile off. I wonder what use could be made of such a country." And the next day he added: "Mosquitos very ferocious this morning." As the two men travelled down Prespatou Creek Milligan noted that "on the main creek and along the numerous small streams running into it or the open poplar slopes there was good growth of grass and soil, and that on top of the benches, whether poplar, spruce or pine, the ground was invariably wet and mossy undoubtedly due to lack of drainage and the clayish soil holding the water." Near the lower end of Prespatou Creek they followed a trail that led southwest to Umbach Creek. During the day Milligan "observed sun for watch error" while that night he "observed Aquilair and Altair for latitude".

During the next few days Milligan explored and surveyed the area around Umbach Creek and along the Blueberry River. On August 5, "after a lunch we again hit the trail back for Nelson trail crossing at Blueberry. Prespatou [the dog] is missing. Pull out from camp without him." The following day they reached the Nelson trail crossing at the Blueberry River where they found Hazen who had returned from Fort St John.

On August 7 Milligan, Cartwright and Hazen packed up all their gear. "Left Blueberry with our seven horses and travelled back over trail to our

Creek crossing on the east side of the North Pine River. This was some of the rugged country that Milligan explored in August during his first survey loop up to the divide between the North Pine and Fort Nelson watersheds. LTSA.

trail at camp crossing on Prespatou Creek. Look ahead on trail for dog but no sign of him." The next day Milligan surveyed the area around the confluence of the Blueberry and North Pine rivers. He noted: "The Blueberry and Pine in these parts flow through deep narrow gorges with precipitous walls of sandstone primarily, great blocks of which in places have broken off and fallen crumbling to the bottom of the canyon." Milligan also wrote: "Tied in the Pine River by track survey with Graham surveys." He connected his track survey with the township surveys that J.R. Graham had made along the northern boundary of the Peace River Block, the only BC government survey in the northern part of the Peace River. Then they "struck across country from the Pine N60°W" and found their trail about three kilometres north of camp. "No sign of our lost dog."

This time Milligan and his crew's route north started up the North Pine River along the east bank. He noted some excellent flats where they crossed the Pine, "openings fringed with poplar and willow clumps." About three kilometres upstream the men crossed a river and continued on a plateau that paralleled the river.

> Muskeg on the plateau, growth of willows, poplar with clumps of spruce, mossy ground. The trail continued the same this PM near the edge of the plateau on the east side of the Pine valley. Although considerably marshy and muskeg land the country, as far as one could see to the east, continued poplar and willow with spruce muskeg. The water from recent rain stays on top of the clayish loam and makes very wet travelling.

Fire-swept flatland, common in the region Milligan explored. LTSA.

On August 11 Milligan finally had the opportunity to report on a decent area of land that he saw.

> Shortly after leaving camp this AM we came upon an excellent stretch of meadow land lying upon a bench 50 ft [15 m] below the upper plateau and stretching probably 1½ mile [2.5 km] westerly to the Pine River. Indians evidently winter their horses here, there being excellent feed, pea vine and grasses.... The greater portion of the country was poplar and willow, also large poplar and occasional spruce and pine. The soil was all good – black where there were willows, otherwise all clayish loam.

Later in the day they "passed through long stretches of poplar and willow country this afternoon which, however, do not appear to extend very far north of the trail and practically upon every occasion one could see out timbered swamps were noted from ¼ to ½ mile off."

That night they camped near a creek that entered the Pine from the north. This was the same creek valley that Milligan had observed when he followed the North Pine south from Nig Creek on August 1. In his diary entry for August 12 Milligan wrote:

> A few miles from camp we branched off the main trail on to one fol-
> lowing northeast up the valley of a large stream 60 feet [18 m] wide by
> 2 or 3 ft [60–90 cm] deep with very dark brown water. Many years ago
> the country has been fire swept (the charred stumps are evidence). Even
> in the muskegs the moss has been burned off and willows and poplar are
> now growing where before was undoubtedly ground similar to the many

Packer Fred Hazen trying to get a horse through some of the boggy area on the summit of the divide between the North Pine and Sikanni Chief rivers. LTSA.

muskegs we encounter in every day's move. Since leaving the vicinity of the Pine the trail followed through dry black pine and poplar with sand soil, being the first day's run with solid footing for some time. Camped at trail crossing of east fork of creek. Observed for time and latitude.

The next day they stopped in the early afternoon at "an Indian camping ground with slough grass feed along creek. The trail branches westerly from here and it was considered advisable not to go on further on account of feed and also one of the horses has contracted a lame foot, evidently sprained in the muskegs." Conditions worsened as the men proceeded north along the valley. Milligan described the country on August 14:

This valley running north and south is about a mile [1.6 km] wide and presented a most desolate appearance as we came out from the pines and onto a small burnt ridge from where we could overlook the lower ground of the valley. In patches the country has been burnt practically clear of all growth – here and there burnt pines standing at odd angles amongst others that have been blown to the ground. A new growth is beginning, small pine a foot [30 cm] high and willows, but not a blade of grass. The only feed for the horses was found along the creek – pickings of slough grass extending a few feet on either side.

9 PM raining with wind from north. The water is already lying in pools and on top of clayish soil (or muck) around our camp.

After an all-night rain the men remained in camp the next day. "The burnt clayish soil around the camp has become very mucky and we had to shift some of the outfit during the night as the puddles were becoming deep. Cartwright fell up to his neck in the creek this morning looking for horses and the rain continues from the north." On August 16 the men resumed their exploration of the valley, but

> the trail was so blocked with windfall and swampy that when we stopped
> for noon (2:30) at the lakes we had gone barely 4 miles [6 km]. The coun-
> try is a rolling jack pine country with nothing else growing but jack pine,
> except in the muskeg where scrub spruce and tamarac are found.... The
> lakes apparently are at a summit. Camp for the night at the lakes as the
> horses are pretty well done up.

Milligan and his crew had now reached the head of this valley and were on the divide between the Peace River and the Fort Nelson River watersheds.

On August 17 Milligan, Cartwright and Hazen travelled through the summit area.

> Made barely 3 miles [5 km] with horses this AM, the muskeg so boggy [it]
> had to be brushed. The trail started northeastly, apparently avoiding bogs
> in vicinity of the lakes and then turned more to the west after crossing
> several of the muskegs draining the summit. Spruce and tamarac prevailed
> in the muskegs while jack pine grew on the ridges in clayish soil. Took 20
> panorama views facing northeast and northwest observing pack train en
> route.
>
> [In the afternoon the trail began] to descend from the summit down
> to a broad low valley, a splendid view of which we could obtain from
> the jack pine ridges. On our way down through the burnt country the
> ground becomes firmer and gravel appears on the surface in places.... The
> entire country except along the edges of the lakes and along the creeks is
> absolutely devoid of grass growth.

The next day, "as we descended, the country showed signs of improvement. Although the entire country had been fire swept there were willows and poplars growing amongst the standing dry trees and windfalls." Milligan found that the trail did not go far down into the valley before heading west and back along the summit. On August 19 the trail they were following proceeded mainly west along the height of land.

> There were several open sandy mounds on top of the hill from which we
> could obtain a splendid view of the country to the north and east (too
> cloudy for photos). As far as the eye could see the country was level with
> exception of a slight roll between summits of creek valleys. To the east,
> probably 50–60 miles [80–100 km] off there was a range of hills running

Burnt country on the summit of the divide between the North Pine and Sikanni Chief rivers. LTSA.

about north and south. We appeared to be higher than country to the north as I could see 2 or 3 different summits one after another. Our trail is very much grown up with dense jack pine growth – also windfalls. The muskeg on top of the hill was boggy and several horses went down time and again.

At their campsite that evening Milligan once more measured the positions of the stars to determine time and latitude.

A fourth day of travel along the summit brought Milligan and his crew to another of the many lakes along the north side of the summit. "The entire country as usual has been fire swept and a second growth of jack pine and willow is now growing.... In places, large patches of jack pine, where only 2 to 3 feet high, had been eaten down by rabbits." Milligan's diary contained a rare mention of nice weather. "Beautiful sunny day."

On August 21 the men started following a trail south back toward the North Pine. "Beavers had dammed the outlet of the lake and a bridge was necessary before the horses could cross. The lake is evidently higher than usual as the trail which follows around the south shore is about a foot under water." Again Milligan took observations for latitude and longitude.

By August 23 Milligan, Cartwright and Hazen were back at the North Pine at a location farther upstream than earlier in the summer. "We left most of our outfit at this point and in the afternoon moved down to our lower cache on the south side of the Pine." (This was their first camp on the river at the beginning of July.) Milligan noted that the trail "was well marked, evidently being considerably travelled by the Indians to reach their hunting country to the north. We found our cache in good order, dry and had not been touched by squirrels." Milligan had completed another loop

One of the numerous lakes on the summit. LTSA.

survey, this time from the North Pine to the north summit of the drainage and the divide between the Peace and Liard watersheds.

The men spent Sunday, August 24 mainly around camp, putting the goods from the cache into packs and preparing for travel. Milligan again measured the stars at night. With the horses carrying heavy loads it took two days for the men to arrive at their upper campsite on the south side of the North Pine River. There they found that the second cache that they had constructed along this river was also in good shape.

While Cartwright and Hazen returned to the lower cache for the remainder of the supplies Milligan worked on the information he had gathered in his surveys and developed his photos in preparation for sending them to the surveyor general.

On August 29 the men "left the cache about noon, forded the Pine and travelled 7 miles [11 km] along the trail to Nelson and camped.... There seemed to be more soil than usual, mostly clayish loam. The country, with exception of timber patches here and there has all been fire swept and grass is now growing." On the last day of August, after it rained all night, Milligan and his crew travelled "up to the summit camping on small muskeg creek with very little feed". Milligan noted that the land was "practically worthless" for agriculture. He and the crew were once again on the divide between the Peace and Fort Nelson watersheds, but this time farther west than they were 10 days before.

The men woke on September 1 to the first snowfall of the season.

Frosty snow fell this morning about light but soon cleared off again and

The view northeast from the summit into the Fort Nelson river drainage. LTSA.

the rest of the day was fair. Last night's frost has started the fall colours to appear in the landscape and leaves on the smaller bushes are falling. We did not go far today, not more than 4½ miles [7 km], as our path lay through dead timber, mostly spruce, a number of which had blown down and blocked our trail.

Milligan commented on the change in vegetation on the north side of the summit: "There was a luxuriant growth of grass, also berries, raspberries principally."

The next day the trail went down into the Conroy Creek valley, a tributary of the Sikanni Chief River. "Along the edge of the creek there are open 6-inch jack pine with sandy loam through which the trail winds on a well beaten track." The weather turned inclement again. It rained all day on September 3, so the men remained in camp, with Milligan working on his surveying calculations. The next day it snowed until noon, although the snow melted as it fell. In the afternoon the men continued on the trail.

The country is undoubtedly improving as we go on, as following northeast down Conroy Creek considerable small poplars and willows are noticed, and the soil is good loamy clay. The large 2-ft [60-cm] dry spruce trees also are evidence of good soil. Fires have devastated practically the whole country with exception of small timbered flats along the creek. On the hills good grass grows amongst windfalls.

In his journal for September 6 Milligan wrote:

Commences raining at 7:30 and continues heavy rain till 2 PM, everything drenched. Had considerable difficulty and were delayed tracing old trail along the river. The old original blazes could be seen at intervals and apparently the first trail kept straight across the flats to the river crossing, and each year as it became blocked by falling timber a new course was taken. Conroy Creek has assumed the proportions of a good sized river about 150 x 3–4 feet [45 x 1 m] deep, and being swift with large boulders is difficult fording for pack horses. We crossed it five times today, crossings within 20–40 chains [400–800 m] of each other. Most shocking windfall – good poplar and large willow flats and timber.

On September 7 the trail left the Conroy Creek valley, heading northwest toward the Sikanni Chief River. The next day the men travelled about 20 kilometres. "The pack horses were seven hours doing the 12 miles [19 km], it being one of the worst stretches of trail we have been over, windfall, boggy muskegs and roots." Milligan had expected to reach the river by now but from their campsite on an open burn ridge he could see a large valley to the north.

On September 9 the men finally arrived at their destination.

We reached the Sikanni Chief River today about 2 PM after travelling about 7 miles [11 km] NW – bad muskeg and windfalls as usual.…The Sikanni at this point lies in a deep depression about 2 miles [3 km] wide on the top and varying from a mile to ½ mile across the timbered flats at the bottom. There is excellent spruce timber on these flats, 2–3 feet in diameter, clean and straight, also numerous large cottonwood.

The unusual high water of last summer flooded the greater part of the flats and it was necessary for us to camp 2 miles from the river to find ground free from damp silty deposits. Indians had camped at river's edge, probably last July after high water. Their bare foot tracks were noticed along the beach. Also, there was evidence of them having made spruce bark canoes. I attempted to ford the river at this point with horse but the water was too deep and swift. The river is about 300 to 400 feet [90–120 m] wide and probably 3-4 [1 m] deep with fairly swift current.

At high water the river flooded all the lower timbered flats. Beautiful day.

Milligan, Cartwright and Hazen spent a day at the site, building a cache and giving the horses a rest. This campsite would be their headquarters for the fall. Since it was a clear day, Milligan began establishing a precise latitude and longitude at this important location in his survey area. He wrote, "Observe for LMT [local meridian time] at 4 PM. The foliage is noticeably changing colour."

Before they could get established at this site the men had to bring the remainder of the supplies from the upper cache on the North Pine. They started back on September 11. "Has been a beautiful day, clear and warm. As we go along I am making another route survey as a check on the first, which I take it, was very erratic as I had to trace out the trail as well as chop

The Sikanni Chief River valley. LTSA.

out windfalls, etc." Since they did not have to cut a trail, Milligan had time not only to survey the route but to take bearings to the prominent hills in the Sikanni Chief valley and to the west. On September 15 the men crossed the summit.

> We travelled about 13 miles [22 km] today. The trail being better than usual, we made it in seven hours. A splendid view of the snow-capped mountains of the Rockies when we reached the summit this morning. It was particularly noticed that we had no frost at camp last night, [but] when we passed over the summit about 2 miles out from camp the muskeg were stiffened with frost, also the water on the trail had coating of ice. Beautifully clear day, gentle southerly and southwest[erly] breeze.

By September 16 they arrived back at their cache and campsite on the North Pine. The following day Hazen left for Fort St John with two horses to get a stove and other necessary items. Frank Beatton, the Hudson's Bay Company factor, recorded in his journal for September 21, "Hazen arrived from the Nelson River for Mr Milligan." He also noted the packer's departure three days later.

Milligan and Cartwright gave their horses a day's rest before packing up and transporting the goods from their cache to the Sikanni Chief. On September 18 Milligan met some Dunne-za people for the first time.

> Left the cache with five horse loads at 11 AM and camped at Ta-ka-tse-ze-tszo-ka Creek (Bear Creek) at 3:30. Soon after we camped rifle shots were heard down the creek followed shortly afterwards by the appearance of 4 or 5 Beaver Indians (Montagneuse and his band). They are camped about a mile from here and evidently heard our horse bells. They seemed

Open country north of the summit between the Sikanni Chief and North Pine rivers. LTSA.

in high spirits, there being a lot of moose in the country, one man having already killed 16 moose. One Indian who seemed of superior intelligence to the others and could talk a little English was more or less interpreter for the others. "Milligan crazy meechee (Mealakan meechee) travel all the time. Nelson country no good, Indian no use horses, all the time muskeg, Nelson, other side. Winter time go all right. He freeze, that muskeg."

Two days later Milligan and Cartwright were once again on the summit. "Southerly breeze all day which increased to gale during the night. Drizzling rain commenced at noon and continued till 3 PM." The next day the two men were delayed for about an hour when one of their horses bogged down in a muddy creek. As they came down Conroy Creek they found that the water level had dropped considerably, making travel easier. On September 26 Milligan and Cartwright arrived back at the Sikanni Chief River where they found everything as they had left it two weeks ago. Milligan was now ready to spend the fall at this location in the valley.

E.B. Hart

On April 8, 1913, Surveyor General George Dawson wrote to E.B. Hart with instructions for his exploration. They were similar to the instructions he gave to Milligan, but not nearly as detailed or technical.

The fact that you are appointed to make this investigation is due to a great extent to the fact that you have already spent time to the west of the area in question and for this reason also it is thought advisable to give you instructions of a general nature…. Confine your examination to the westerly portion of the district, your boundaries being roughly to the north, the north boundary of the province, the west, the range of mountains lying east of the valley of the Kechika River, supposed to be the main range of the Rockies, to the south the 57th parallel of latitude and to the east, the watershed of the Fort Nelson River.

This region adjoined Milligan's surveys to the east, Frank Swannell's surveys to the south and the area to the west that Hart had reported on in 1912. As he had instructed Milligan, the surveyor general told Hart: "The country which has been assigned to you is almost totally unknown and you must bear this in mind when making reports and you must make these as full and comprehensible as possible." He asked for accurate maps of the land's physical features and for a report on the economic potential of the region. Like Milligan, Hart was to take daily barometer and thermometer readings and to keep a diary. "This, I may say, is following the practice of land surveyors employed by this department," wrote Dawson. He also ordered Hart to send reports from the field whenever possible and to make a final report after he returned in the fall of 1914.

Dawson also wrote to the manager of the Hudson's Bay Company in Victoria informing him of Hart's exploration and arranging for some assistance: "I would esteem it a favour if you would advise your factors in the northern country that this department will pay them for any supplies or provisions which Mr Hart may require during this period." He also said: "Mr Hart has no party with him and he may require the services of an Indian canoeman or packer and the department will be prepared to recoup the Hudson's Bay Co. for any disbursements which they make in assisting Mr Hart to secure such services." Carrying a copy of this letter and one from Provincial Secretary Henry Young, Hart departed from Victoria in mid April 1913.

The surveyor general's difficulties with Hart began almost immediately. Hart was supposed to purchase a sextant from surveyor R.P. Bishop for measuring latitude. Bishop wrote to Dawson:

In accordance with your instructions, I have supplied Mr E.B. Hart, explorer, with my three-inch sextant. I was unable to get in touch with Mr Hart until an hour before his departure. He had not enough money to pay me and being very busy considering the advisability of taking a book of tables and a nautical almanac was unable to come over to the department. I enclose his receipt for the instrument.

Frank Swannell ended up with the instrument and reflected on it and Hart in a letter he wrote in 1934: "Strange to say, I have the sextant bought for him. It bears no evidence of use – when he got up there he found he couldn't use it, having neglected to bring an artificial horizon."

The most expeditious route for Hart to follow to reach the western area of his exploration was to go to Telegraph Creek, then follow the Hudson's Bay Company transportation route through Dease Lake to the Liard River and proceed overland to the Kechika River valley. Hart knew this route from the years that he had spent working in the area. But instead, he decided to travel by way of Atlin. This route may have been in deference to Dr Young, who was a resident of this community. It also appears that Hart was trying to avoid the Telegraph Creek and Dease Lake area.

Hart described his journey to Atlin. "Leaving Victoria on April 19th, 1913, I took steamer from Seattle to Skagway, and the White Pass Railway from there to Cariboo, thence by stage to Atlin." He stayed at the Royal Hotel for a few days. With the assistance of J.A. Fraser, the government agent in Atlin, he procured supplies and equipment worth $212.65 from several merchants in the community: clothing from Thomas James; food supplies and dog packs from E.L. Pillman; dog harness, dishes and outfit from J.B. Kershaw; a dog from Konrad Wawrecka; dogs, snowshoes and sled from J.H. Senn; and transportation and supplies from Louis Schulz. Fraser wrote to the surveyor general that he paid these expenses: "Taking the liberty of doing so on the strength of your letter to the Hudson's Bay Company which he showed me and of the communication which he had from the Honourable Dr Young. Mr Hart represented that he had only a limited supply of currency and would need it later on when he could not secure further funds."

On April 28 Hart wrote to Dawson that he was leaving Atlin that day.

I intend to follow the Yukon Telegraph line as far as the Nahlin 125 miles [200 km] and then, if it is possible to strike across country to the foot of Dease Lake. The weather has turned soft and I shall probably have some difficulty with soft snow but I hope to get through by that route, as it will cut off about 150 miles [240 km].

I have had the usual amount of difficulty in outfitting here, but thanks to Mr Fraser's, the Gold Commissioner, assistance, I now have a good outfit of four dogs, sleigh, etc., and should make good time.

I should like, if it is possible, to have the Nautical Almanac for 1914 forwarded to use at the Hudson's Bay post, Fort Nelson River, as soon as it is obtainable. The almanac which I got from Hibben's before leaving did not give the parallax and I found it necessary to get that on the ship coming up.

Also, may I ask that when reports are received from me, 75% of my salary should be placed to my credit at the Canadian Bank of Commerce, Victoria.

Although Hart claimed his route saved him distance, it was a much more difficult and dangerous journey. Nevertheless, it brought him to the foot of

Dease Lake while, avoiding the Hudson's Bay Company posts at Telegraph Creek and Dease Lake, even though he had the surveyor general's letter authorizing payment for supplies purchased from the HBC.

Hart's next letter to Dawson was from McDame Creek on the Dease River a month later.

> I have been very considerably delayed by the backwardness of the season – the small lakes on the river being still frozen and I found it necessary to chop ice and break my way through them. I have also been bothered a good deal by snow blindness which has left my eyes very weak for the time being.
>
> In crossing Dease Lake I had a very narrow escape from losing the entire outfit; the dogs being out on a sheet of thin ice through which I expected at every moment to see dogs and sleigh disappear. I broke passage up to them in a boat and just caught the sleigh by one finger as it went down. As it was I lost my shaft dog, the biggest and strongest of the team.
>
> I have also lost two other dogs from sickness – some epidemic which appears to be prevalent. I have another one sick which I hope to pull through.
>
> I have decided that, in place of leaving the Dease River here for the Kechika as originally intended, I shall go down the Dease River to a point on the Liard River 10 miles [16 km] below the Liard Post and strike southeast from there for the Fort Nelson post direct. The snow between here and the Kechika is still deep and there are two very bad rivers to cross, all which I shall avoid by taking the more northerly route, as well as being able to take in a new section all the way over.

Hart's return to the area attracted some attention. Before leaving McDame Creek, he wrote a second letter to the surveyor general:

> I have found it necessary to give my own cheque for the sum of $337.00 in favour of Messrs Hyland & Belfry in connection with a personal matter. I shall also find it necessary to issue another for $50.00.
>
> When I left Victoria my financial affairs were such that at the present time I don't know where there are a few thousand to my credit, or not sufficient to meet these cheques.
>
> I have written to the Manager of the Bank of Commerce asking him to notify you should there not be sufficient funds, and if you can arrange in some manner to have these met, it will be of great value to me.
>
> I've been having jolly rough luck so far, more especially with my dogs and snow blindness, but I hope the worst of the troubles are over now and it will be pretty plain sailing from now on.

During his travels through the area, probably at Lower Post, Hart used his letter from the HBC to obtain a cash advance. The Victoria office then requested payment from the surveyor general, citing Dawson's letter from April.

Hart travelled down the Dease River to Lower Post near the junction of the Dease and Liard rivers. In his government report he wrote:

> There were no Indians at the post when I arrived and I spent a number of days here endeavouring to obtain all the information possible concerning the country lying to the east, and also to obtain an Indian to accompany me. This latter I found extremely difficult, as there appeared to be very few Indians indeed who knew anything of the country, and those few who had been across appeared to be very unwilling to undertake a long journey, especially in view of the fact that they would have to return alone.

Eventually Hart hired two First Nations men named Barney and Charley, and the three departed from Lower Post on June 26. It was now more than two months since he had left Victoria, and Hart still had not reached the area where he was to begin his exploration. He reported to the surveyor general from Fort Nelson.

> The distance between the Liard Post and the Fort Nelson Post is some 325 miles [520 km], not taking into account the various side trips made up various forks and tributaries. I have taken careful sextant observations for latitude at numerous points and for longitude on principal divides, which latter observations must necessarily be very approximate only, as I am compelled to rely upon an ordinary watch for time….
>
> Under separate cover will be found a number of films which I am sending out to be developed. It would perhaps be well to advise the photographer who does the work that these films are taken with a Goerz 'Tenax', and that in all probability the majority are over-exposed, as they were not likely to be developed for a very considerable time after exposure.

From Liard Post, Barney and Charley led Hart along a traditional First Nations trail to the Kechika River in the broad Rocky Mountain Trench, on the west side of the Rocky Mountains. Although he was not yet in the area described by the surveyor general, the Kechika River valley was as far east as Hart had travelled in 1912. After rafting the Kechika, Hart's route went southeast, crossing the Rabbit River on July 3, one week after leaving Liard Post. "Leaving the Rabbit River one climbs steadily, from ridge to ridge, moss covered with scrub pine and tamarac, to an altitude of 3700 feet [1130 m], and after travelling nearly 20 miles [32 km], the head of a small creek is reached, which creek forms the west head of the Riviere des Vents or Wind River as it is always termed here."

Hart and his guides continued southeast. They rejoined the Rabbit River "and found it to be still a fairly large river running in a wide valley. Some

The Rabbit River. E.B. Hart photograph; LTSA file 6952S.

2 miles [3 km] above this point the river forks, one coming from the east and one from the southeast of about equal length". Hart proceeded up the valley of the southeast fork to a

> divide at an altitude of 4000 feet [1200 m], and running S.35°E. from here starts a tributary of the Trout River down a very steep and gloomy ravine. Here one fairly enters the main range of the Rockies, high rugged limestone peaks appearing in front, some of them reaching an altitude of fully 7000 feet [2100 m].
>
> Until one has seen it, one can form no conception of the luxuriant vegetation of these mountain passes, and the wonderful variety of flowers which form a carpet under one's feet at these high altitudes. The timber line on this slope is evidently lower than on the western as there appears to be no timbers above 3500 feet [1000 m].

Hart spent about three and a half weeks exploring the area between the Rocky Mountains and Fort Nelson. He followed a branch of the Trout River down to Muncho Lake. "Almost at the same point another fork comes in from the south, up which fork I travelled to its head.... Crossing the divide at the head of the east fork of the Trout River at an altitude of 2500 feet [750 m] one descends a small creek for about 6 miles [10 km] to the Toad River."

For the first time Hart wrote ecstatically about the conditions of an area he was exploring.

Crossing the river on a raft and following it down one finds the mountains approaching the river very closely for about 14 miles [23 km], leaving no bottom or bench land, though on the bends, where there is a gravel bar, very fine spruce and poplar grows. Here I fancy that I found the wild honeysuckle. Below this, however, the high mountains appear to give out and here one finds some 3 to 4000 acres [1200–1600 ha] of land covered with tall straight spruce and poplar, averaging probably 10,000 feet to the acre [7500 m/ha] The timbered land has rich alluvial soil and would be first rate farming land when cleared, as the altitude is only 1350 feet [400 m] In addition I estimate there are 4000 acres [1600 ha] of grass covered hillsides suitable for grazing and several hundred acres of clear meadow land fit for hay or crops. On the opposite side of the river there is an equal quantity of land which has been burnt off some years back and is now first class farming land.

Between the Toad River (Tsaheh Daisah in Indian) and its principal fork, the Chlas-teel-tua [Racing River] which enters it 8 miles [12 km] above its mouth the first two miles are rolling hills or rather undulations of grazing land. Open poplar time, poplar (not cottonwood) up to 15 inches [40 cm] in diameter, standing at wide intervals, no underbrush, with pine grass, bunch grass, pea vine, vetches and lupines. There are here at least 3500 or 4000 acres [1400–1600 ha], possibly more, of splendid grazing land, running down the Toad and across to the Chlas-teel-tua. The next 4 miles [6 km] are the finest stretch of perfect farming land that I have seen for a great number of years. A level stretch of entirely clear meadow, not a stick on it, a clear creek running through it, no gravel, pea vine up to one's waist. Altitude 1250 feet [380 m]. Six inches [15 cm] of snow in winter. Hills on either side up to 300 feet [90 m] affording grazing.

In his official report to the government Hart wrote: "I had not hoped to find such a beautiful section of agricultural land, and land suitable for cattle raising so close in to the high mountains. There are here, in all, on both sides of the river, at a conservative estimate, 300,000 acres [120,000 ha] of bottom lands, low benches and undulating country." Perhaps thinking back to his years in the East Kootenay region Hart also wrote, incorrectly: "For the first time east of the Kechika River the bull, or yellow pine, is found on the slopes facing south and east, and upon nearing the Toad River there are about 25,000 acres [10,000 ha] of open grass-covered benches of scattered bull pine and burnt timber."

Although Hart's estimation of the potential of the Toad River valley was optimistic, there has been considerable agricultural development in the area since the construction of the Alaska Highway. In the valleys of both the Toad and Racing rivers there are some ranches where hay is grown, and there is also some pasture land for horses. At one time cattle were raised in the Toad River valley, but high transportation costs made this uneconomical. The tradition of range burning, noted by Hart, continues today.

Hart crossed the Chlas-teel-tua "by raft in very swift, white water, and where I nearly lost my outfit". He followed "the east branch of this river to its headwaters, over a divide, and down into the Ta-dzah [Tetsa] River". From the lower section he headed east toward the Muskwa River.

Before reaching this river, however, it was necessary to climb a steep ridge to a height of 3650 feet [1100 m], which was well repaid when I found myself on the top of an extraordinary sandstone escarpment, apparently not more than a mile in width, perfectly flat-topped running north and south along course of Sikanni [Muskwa]. Looking across the valley to the south of the east and distant possibly 40 miles [64 km], the same flat-topped clean-cut escarpment is seen, with the Sikanni River coming from the south in between. From this point the most wonderful view imaginable is presented. Behind one to the west the high, snow peaks of the Rockies running N30°W., through which one has just come. To the south a spur of high snow peaks in the distance running east and west in which and behind which the Sikanni, the Prophet and the Fort Nelson head, to the north the low country towards and across the Liard River with no mountains between, except for an occasional outcrop of the sandstone ridge, and to the east and north of east, the Sikanni River running slightly north of east to its junction with the Fort Nelson River some 50 miles [80 km] distant. The most splendid picture I have ever seen.

When Hart and his guides reached the river they made a raft and floated down the river to Fort Nelson.

10 miles [16 km] above the Fort Nelson post, a large tributary, the Prophet River, comes in. This river practically parallels the Sikanni and from what I can learn at present heads in almost the same mountain.

Upon reaching Fort Nelson post I found to my surprise that I had not been travelling on the Fort Nelson River, as I had supposed, but upon the Sikanni – which river I had been looking for a fortnight and which I had given up entirely.

On August 2 they arrived at Fort Nelson. Hart wrote enthusiastically about the resources he saw around the post.

From what was told me by Mr MacLeod, who has been manager at this post for the past eight years, there is no question at all either as to the fertility of the soil or suitability of the climate for agriculture. I had very fine large-sized new potatoes shown me and saw corn in the milk in the garden, and Mr MacLeod tells me that anything at all that has been tried does splendidly. Beans, corn, cucumbers, tomatoes have all been tried here and barley and oats have also been tested successfully. As the altitude

William Cartwright on a hill above Fort Nelson looking up the Muskwa River valley. LTSA.

The Naming of a River

The Muskwa River is a large tributary of the Fort Nelson River, joining it just upstream from the Hudson's Bay Company post. In the early maps of the area, including the BC government's 1912 map, it was called the Sikanni River. Farther south, the Sikanni Chief and Fontas rivers join to form the Fort Nelson River. In a letter to the surveyor general in January 1914, Hart wrote:

> The only name the Indians recognize (and there are no other people) is the Musquah. The custom apparently is for a separate band of the Sikanni Indians to hunt on each of these rivers, and the rivers receive the names of the leaders in each band. Thus we have Musquah's River, the Prophet's River, the Sikanni Chief's River and Fantasque's River....
> The Fort Nelson river above the post is known as the Sikanni, so in order to avoid confusion we [Hart and Milligan] have decided, subject to your approval, to call the river now called Sikanni Chief, and each of the others by the above mentioned name. This river, of course, must remain unchanged as the Fort Nelson.

The Muskwa is on the edge of the territories explored by Hart and surveyed by Milligan. While Hart spells the name "Musquah" on his sketch of the area, Milligan uses "Muskwa" (the current spelling) on his map.

cannot be much over 800 feet [250 m] (I did not stay long enough to test barometers) and there is no frost, added to the undoubted fertility of the alluvial soil, there can be no doubt that here, on this Sikanni, Prophet and Fort Nelson rivers lies the largest body and perhaps the finest body of agricultural land remaining to the Province.

As to the timber, there is no question. It is undoubtedly the finest spruce and cottonwood in all northern British Columbia, and it will be a very big task to estimate its area and quantity. In this connection it appears to me that some serious effort should be made to impress upon the Indians in this section the criminal nature of their custom of burning off timber to make moose pasture. It is a very difficult matter, as these Indians are all Stick Indians, living in the hills and speaking no English, but no crime so great can be imagined as that this magnificent timber, extending far up the Fort Nelson, Prophet and Sikanni Rivers, down to the mouth of the Fort Nelson and both up and down the Liard River should in any way be destroyed.

Hart wrote a letter to McDonald Egnell, the HBC factor at Lower Post, and had one of his guides deliver it. He knew Egnell, a long-time HBC employee, from his years at Dease Lake.

Dear Mac. Got here all right after usual kind of trip with two Siwashes. Might have been better, might have been worse. Very poor, worthless country until one gets this side of mountains and not very much here.... I'm enclosing boys' accounts for you to settle for me. They've blown in about $50.00 apiece, out of the balance you ought to be able to collect your jawbone.

A *jawbone* was a credit that the Hudson's Bay Company advanced to trusted people, usually through goods purchased. The HBC often gave jawbones to trappers before the beginning of trapping season, which would be repaid with furs brought in at the end of the season. The jawbone played an important role in the HBC's barter economy. Before Egnell would pay Barney and Charley their wages, he would deduct the expenses listed by Hart along with any jawbone they owed him at Lower Post. Using the authority of his letter from the surveyor general, Hart authorized Egnell to pay his guides for 38 days of work and 20 days of return trip. From this he was to deduct their expenses at Fort Nelson – $52 for Barney and $41.50 for Charley.

Hart encountered more difficulties at Fort Nelson, which he described to the surveyor general:

To my very great astonishment and dismay, I find on reaching this Post, that in spite of the explicit assurance of the Hudson's Bay Co.'s Manager in Edmonton, given to me by wire before leaving Victoria, that all ordinary supplies for two men could be obtained at this Post, and although the boat-load of year's trade goods arrived only five days before me, yet no supplies, other than tea, are obtainable. This, and the lower river and Liard, are not sections in which one can depend entirely on one's rifle – and if one could, no cartridges are to be had – and for the coming winter it is an absolute necessity that supplies for oneself and dogs be somehow obtained. The Post Inspector happens to be here in the absence of the Post Manager, and he advises me that my only chance is to go down by canoe to Fort Simpson and obtain there all that I am able, and also take the opportunity of forwarding these papers etc. – which of course I presume I will be compelled to take, though I shall have to make the journey, some 300 miles [500 km] downstream from here alone, as no canoe men are to be obtained. The time will not be all wasted, as I had planned, if all went well, to have made a thorough examination of the lower Nelson and Liard Rivers this Fall, and I hope still to be able to do that.

The expenses so far have been, to my mind, very great, but I venture to assure you, quite unavoidable, if I was to hope to do work of any value and get report out to you this fall.

I sincerely trust, however, that the heaviest expenses have been met, and that outside of the expense of my enforced journey to Ft Simpson and return, the expense account for men, guides etc. will be of a very trifling nature. I assure you that I shall use my best endeavours to make them so.

I learn that a winter mail starts from Edmonton on Dec. 1st, arriving at this Post some time next February, and there are a certain number of small articles which I shall need very badly and which would be of very great assistance to me if forwarded to me at ... Fort Nelson Post, Fort Nelson River, Mackenzie District, in the care of the H.B. Co. by that mail.

1. Browne's Nautical Almanac for 1914.

2. Good diary 1914. One with two pages each day preferred.

3. If possible – Artificial Horizon – Am using at present open iron tray & am absolutely at the mercy of every puff of wind.

4. Very strong magnifying glass. Have very small sextant, and as eye is injured by snow blindness, I find it difficult to read the viewer, even with strong glass on instrument.

5. Good pair of yellow-tinted snow glasses. Those allowing no white light to enter around sides.

6. Tube of ink pellets for fountain pen.

7. Chart of compass variations.

8. Obtain for me the exact latitude and longitude of Fort Nelson Post, fixed by Ogilvie, that I may have one fixed point to check up time by.

9. Some section paper. All of mine was ruined by water in raft accident.

I have stated above that as no supplies were to be obtained at Fort Nelson I should probably be compelled to get boys and go down to Fort Simpson to try to get an outfit. Since writing the above, finding it impossible to get Indians at Fort Nelson, I bought a small spruce bark canoe and came down alone to Fort Liard, where I obtained two canoemen and came on down to Fort Simpson, where I arrived this morning and where I find I will be able to get sufficient supplies. On my way down I heard that Mr Milligan was expected in at Fort Nelson and that he was counting on wintering there. He will probably find it necessary, as I have, to come down here; and as supplies are short here, may possibly have to winter here.

On August 14 Hart wrote to the surveyor general from Fort Simpson:
There is one matter which is troubling me beyond all others and robbing this work of all the pleasure which it would otherwise have for me, and that is expense. I appear, ever since I started, to have been forced into positions where I simply had to spend money in order to get ahead, and now on the top of it has come this unlooked for trip to the Mackenzie River for supplies.

Always there is present this fear that the Minister will be objecting to the expense account, which makes one hurry over ground which one would otherwise spend more time on – simply to save money.

I am now about to purchase supplies sufficient to put me through the next twelve months and I hope there will be no more outlay on that score. I have arranged with the chief man of the Sikanni tribe, in whose country I shall be this winter, to post me as to his district, and go with me if necessary, at any time, and the expense will be trifling there.

Next summer, if all goes well, I will be on the headwaters of the Rabbit R. and don't count on spending any money there – apart perhaps from getting some stuff taken over there in the spring. You may be certain that I shall not spend a dollar that I can avoid, and if you could send me a line by the winter mail, giving me some assurance regarding this matter it would be a great relief to me.

If this work which I do here is satisfactory what do you think of setting the wheels in motion to get a permit from Ottawa for me to shoot a specimen of the Wood Buffalo for the Victoria Museum?

There is one thing which I omitted from my official letter. I shall need 200 cartridges for my rifle. 30 U.S. 1903 Model. 100 soft-point and 100 Long-Range Spitzer bullet. Can you arrange to have them sent in to me? It might be possible to have them brought by winter mail, but if not, by the steamer next summer, though I should need them before then.

Also, will you kindly see that $40.00 is forwarded in my name to the Secretary of the Royal Geographical Society? I think that's all I have to

trouble you with for now, except to write out a formal request to have money paid up to Bank. Anxiously awaiting to hear from you to writer.
Yours faithfully,
E.B. Hart

After sending out his letters, report and other items Hart returned up-river with his supplies for fall and the winter, assisted by two "Indian boys [to] help track the canoe back up the river". Tracking the heavily loaded canoe up the Liard and Fort Nelson rivers required three people: two on shore pulling with ropes, one tied to the bow and the other to the stern, and one in the canoe paddling and steering it. Hart and his assistants would have had to track the canoe in parts of the river that had strong current.

Hart commented on the changing landscape in a letter to the surveyor general:

> That the whole country is drying up, and drying very rapidly, is beyond all question. Twenty-five years ago, which is not a very long time, the Mackenzie River steamboat drew 5 feet [1.5 m] of water. Today it is found necessary to build them to draw not more than 2½ feet. When Mr McConnell came down the Liard River in 1887 or '88, he speaks of the Dease River above the Liard Post as running through a "dreary inhospitable waste". Ice was visible in the river banks in the soil even in August. Today, any one passing down that river in May will see thousands of acres of splendid, dry land covered with bunch and other grasses.

Hart arrived back at Fort Nelson on September 6. He finished the summer of 1913 by making a short trip up the Kledo Creek valley, following

> the trail which had been made and used in 1898 by a few prospectors who had made their way across through the Hay River country with horses to Fort Nelson, and had been guided west from there by the Indians up the tributary of the Muskwa called the Kled-oh-sthlin....

> On the slopes facing the Muskwa, and in the valley of the Kled-oh-sthlin, there will be found approximately 75,000 acres [30,000 ha] of dry bench land which has been burnt over in the past and cleared of timber, and which is now covered with a good growth of bunch grass and would afford capital grazing for cattle, and upon which it is possible in a favourable season to winter horses.

Volunteer Correspondents

Among the items Hart sent to the surveyor general from Fort Simpson in August was a flower collection. In a letter sent with the flowers to John Davidson, the provincial botanist, on October 14, Dawson noted the condition of the plants (and probably Hart's lack of experience in collecting flowers). "I enclose some botanical specimens sent to me by Mr E.B. Hart from the extreme north-easterly portion of the province. They have doubtless travelled many miles by Indian packers before reaching mail communication. Should any specimen be of particular interest, I should be obliged if you would advise me."

Born in Scotland, Davidson had been the curator of the botany museum at the University of Aberdeen until he and his family immigrated to Canada in 1911, moving to Vancouver where his sister lived. While searching for employment, Davidson met with Henry Young, the provincial secratary and proposed conducting a botanical survey of the province. Young created a provincial botanical office with Davidson as assistant. The following year Davidson became provincial botanist. One of his objectives was "to assemble a representative collection of plants from all parts of the province". Davidson had only a small staff and could not travel around the province gathering plants, so he enlisted "volunteer correspondents" to collect plants and send them to his office. With Young's permission Davidson sent a letter to teachers around the province encouraging them to become involved, and many did so.

Because the surveyor general had many survey crews working in remote areas of the province, Davidson had asked him in early 1913 to help get more specimens from "out-of-the-way regions such as Cariboo and northern BC". Men on several survey crews served as volunteer correspondents for Davidson in 1913 and 1914 including T.H. Taylor during his survey of northwestern BC in 1913, and George Copley, Frank Swannell's assistant, who collected plants in northern BC in 1913 and 1914.

Davidson replied immediately to the surveyor general thanking him for sending the plants from Hart.

> On looking through them I see quite a number of interesting specimens, some of which have not previously been sent to this office and with which I am not familiar.
>
> A few of those which seem most interesting unfortunately suffer for a lack of material, the specimens being rather scrappy.
>
> I think it will be necessary for me to write out a small pamphlet giving a few hints on field collecting, such as might be useful for the

One of the plants Hart collected. It was identified as a subspecies of *Rubus arcticus*, commonly known as Dwarf Nagoonberry, similar to wild raspberries. The notes at the bottom of the card indicate examinations by botanists in 1949, 1969 and 2009. Beaty Biodiversity Museum V32461.

members of your staff. Perhaps during the winter I may find time to do this, so that you can let them have copies before next season.

I trust that the specimens may be retained for our herbarium where desired, so they will be valuable for us to have to supplement our records.

The flora as represented by this collection is certainly very different from the flora further south, and contains one or two unexpected plants.

I cannot in the meantime say if there are any new or doubtful species, until I have examined those plants which are new to me.

On November 10 the surveyor general wrote to Davidson:

Mr Hart is spending the next year in the extreme north portion of the province and should you have any suggestions to make in regard to what class of specimens you wish collected, possibly the only chance of communicating with Mr Hart will be in the immediate future as the next mail leaves Athabasca Landing for Fort Simpson on the 1st December. If you write to Mr Hart in the next two or three days I will be pleased to forward the letter.

I must ask you to bear in mind the fact that Mr Hart is travelling alone and has not the facilities for taking care of specimens so you must not expect any great results from him. There are, however, possibly

certain matters in connection with which you are specially desirous of
obtaining information and for this reason I suggest your writing.

Davidson responded immediately to the surveyor general's suggestion.

Thank you for the opportunity afforded for communicating with Mr
Hart regarding botanical survey work in the N.E. part of the province.
I enclose a communication for Mr Hart, and have left the envelope un-
sealed so that you may see what suggestions I had to offer. I trust I have
not exceeded the privilege you gave me, and that you are agreeable to
Mr Hart adopting the suggestions.

Although botanical survey work is primarily of scientific importance, I think that its economic importance is often overlooked. A collection of specimens from a selected area is to the botanist, what a meteorological chart is to the meteorologist. From it he can tell something
of the climate, exposure, length of growing season in that area, and is
able to form an opinion as to its value for agricultural or arboricultural
purposes....

As the vast majority of plants in BC differ from those in Europe, it
is first of scientific, and later of economic importance to ascertain the
relation of our native flora to its environment, so that our successors
may use this information for the future welfare of the Province, just as
similar knowledge is utilized in Europe.

Last April Mr T.H. Taylor BCLS called at the Botanical Office and
obtained information regarding the collecting and preservation of
plants from the Ground Hog country. I noted he was surprised at the
simplicity and portability of our plant pressers and I understand he was
to take one up with him....

Enclosed please find a list of the plants, from E.B. Hart, forwarded
by you to this office on Oct 14. Again thanking you....

Davidson's 1913 government report included a section called "Co-
operation of Volunteer Correspondents" in which he mentioned Hart's
work.

Mr E.B. Hart, through the surveyor general, G.H. Dawson, Esq., sent
in an interesting collection of specimens illustrating the flora of the
north-east portion of British Columbia, which has hitherto been
unexplored. He is spending the winter in this region so as to be able
to commence work early in spring, and it is expected that as a result of
his work during the upcoming seasons a fairly good knowledge of the
flora of this outlying portion of the Province will be obtained.

Hart received Davidson's letter and suggestions in the spring of 1914
and in a letter to the surveyor general said, "I can't help wondering
whether he fancies I'm travelling with a furniture van – and a list of

names – botanical of course – of the plants I sent out last year. As I regret to say I have never made a study of botany, with three or four exceptions his list does not contain much of value to me."

Despite his response, Hart once more collected plants for Davidson in the summer of 1914. In February 1915 the provincial botanist sent Hart a letter of thanks, and said, "the most interesting feature of the flora of that region – according to the plants submitted – is the great similarity to our characteristic coast flora. Fifty per cent represent species which are common along the coast of the mainland and on Vancouver Island." Davidson also noted the absence of characteristic dry-belt plants.

After the provincial botanist office was disbanded in 1916 the plants collected by Davidson went to the University of British Columbia and today are housed in the offices of the Beaty Biodiversity Museum. Some of the plants that Hart collected still remain. Because the area where Hart collected is at the edge of several ecological zones, scientists from all over the world have studied Hart's collection of plants that lived a century ago in northern BC.

Fall 1913

George Milligan's first day at his fall camp was sunny, so he took an observation for local meridian time. In the late morning Cartwright left with the horses to bring up the remaining supplies from the cache on the North Pine River. That afternoon, Milligan hiked along the hilltops on the south side of the valley and took photos of the area. "Carty returns at 3:30 and reports one of his horses bogged 5 miles back and can't possibly get him out. Both of us then return and work on the animal till dark when we finally get him out after much lifting and scratching, and go 2 miles further on and camp (pitch dark)."

The next morning, September 28, the "horses hit the trail for the Pine and not until 11 does Carty return with them." While Cartwright was rounding up the horses, Milligan met some Sekani people for the first time.

> After Cartwright left, I heard some humans talking, laughing, and kids
> squeaking about ½ mile to the south. Shortly afterwards a Sikannie Indian
> with gun over shoulder stalked up to the tent. He seemed quite affable
> and pleased with himself, and to show disposition to be friendly shook
> hands with me. He spoke very little English but by signs and grunts I
> managed to get information about the river and trail to Fort Nelson. His
> pack train of klootches [women], kids and dogs passed the camp.

In the afternoon, Cartwright resumed his trip to the North Pine while Milligan returned to camp. The Sekani arrived the following day, camping at the edge of the river. "Trade tea, 'soo gah', 'plouse' for moose meat.... Gain much useful information from the Indian today. He makes sketches of streams, trails, etc., in the sand."

Milligan also began constructing a canoe. He wrote to the surveyor general: "A canoe was made when in camp on the Sikanni Chief and it is proposed, next spring, to make a trip to Hay Lakes by going up Fantasque [Fontas] River and across a short portage to Hay River." He found a suitable

First Nations women packers, probably Sekani. RBCM LS367.

cottonwood tree and cut it down, then devoted much of the next 10 days to building the canoe. On October 4 he noted in his diary, "my cottonwood log is now assuming the shape of a canoe", and on the following day that he was "pleased with its appearance." When not working on the canoe he developed four rolls of photographs, traded with the Sekani for moccasins★ and gloves, spent time working on his field notes, and prepared his report to the surveyor general to go with the last mail of the fall.

On October 9 "Indian Bellyful comes to camp with whitefish from Fish Lake [Klua Lakes]. Reports the river too low for canoe." Milligan had taken pleasure and pride in the construction of his canoe, but Bellyful's simple comment was a reminder that this was not a practical means of transportation. As Milligan would learn, the traditional First Nations means of transportation on the rivers of the area was by spruce bark canoe, which was quick and easy to make and could be used in shallow water.

On October 12 Milligan had an unexpected visitor. "Hart arrives in camp about 4 PM with Indian boy. He has 3 dogs and came from Fort Nelson. Much comparing of notes and discussion – and cursing 'our vast empire'."

★ These were probably calf-length moccasins made of moose hide and tied with string. Milligan likely wore them over wool socks. Moccasins would have been lighter, warmer and more flexible than his boots, and they would dry quicker. He carried several so he would always have a dry pair to put on.

Drawing a map in sand. RBCM LS368.

In his government report, Hart described his movements that eventually led him to Milligan's camp. In early October he left Fort Nelson, heading south by way of the Klua Lakes, where the post obtained its fish in winter.

> On the Klua Creek, a small creek which runs out of the Klua Lake into the Fort Nelson River, there are approximately 30,000 acres [12,000 ha] of good bench land, all of which has been cleared of timber by fire and which is capable at the present time of supporting a large number of cattle, as several thousand acres are quite clear of any growth of time and are covered with grass standing 4 feet [1.2 m] high, which could be cut for hay for winter feed.
>
> Klua Lake itself is a small lake about 5 miles [8 km] in length and not more than a mile wide, from which large numbers of the finest whitefish I have ever seen in the north are obtained by the Indians and dried and frozen for dog feed and their own sustenance in the winter months.

In his report to the surveyor general in January 1914 he wrote:

> This fall I travelled over the country between this post [Fort Nelson] and

what are known as the Fish Lakes.... As will be seen from the accompanying rough sketch, the country is very largely muskeg and 2nd growth and rolling hills, with one fairly large block of good grazing and in parts agricultural land.... From the Fish Lakes to the Sikanni Chief River most of the land is either muskeg or rolling hills covered with 2nd-growth pine and spruce.

While Hart was at Klua Lake he learned that "two white men had come in with horses" and were camped on the Sikanni Chief River about 60 kilometres away. He travelled over to the river and found Milligan there. "As it was impossible at that time of year, rivers not yet having frozen, to travel with any great advantage, I decided to join forces with Mr Milligan, and so moved my camp over ... and remained there until Christmas time, when we all moved in to Fort Nelson post."

On October 14 Milligan wrote in his diary: "Hart travels back to Fish Lake and I hit back trail to meet pack train and run across them five miles out and travel back with them to camp. Fred takes horses back again to feed on top of hill. Horses weary and poor. They brought everything except some sugar and jam which was cached 12 miles [20 km] back."

Milligan's crew spent the next three days arranging the supplies Hazen and Cartwright brought as well as preparing for Hazen's final trip back to Fort St John. Milligan spent much of his time writing letters and preparing material for the surveyor general. On October 17 he wrote a personal letter to George Dawson to go with his report.

> Our packer starts back today with our six horses for Fort St John where they will winter, and I am forwarding by him report with plan, also two packages of photo films. I had hoped to forward mail by the Treaty party during the summer; they, however, didn't travel this way but reached Nelson from the north. It will be seen from my sketch plan that up to the present time we have not covered very much country. Travel over the trails with these horses has been necessarily slow. We were unable to secure a guide of any sort and the trails not being travelled very much, even by the Indians, were in places grown over and blocked with windfall, being very difficult to follow.
>
> I was misinformed by the HB Company manager at Victoria in regard to the Fort Nelson post, it being abandoned for only a few months during the summer when the trader goes down the river with his fur. It is fortunate, however, that we brought in our own supplies, as practically nothing can be obtained from the post, their trading stock consisting of tea and a little flour. We have enough supplies with us now to last the winter and next summer....
>
> So far it has been a most disappointing country, fully 75% of it being marshy – mostly muskeg – and I am told that the whole of this vast region

is the same – all burnt over muskegs. There is some good timber along the river bottoms being mostly spruce and cottonwood, the extent of which is being carefully noted as we go along.

On October 18 Milligan took his mail and accompanied Hazen back on the Fort Nelson trail to where the horses had been left. There he made a sad discovery. "Find Croppy dead." Croppy was a horse that had worked on his and J.H. Gray's crews for many years. The two men camped overnight with five centimetres of fresh snow on the ground, and the next morning, "Fred leaves camp with the six horses and starts back for St John. I travel back to camp at Sikanni – see fresh tracks of moose and bear."

The next day a warm chinook wind melted the snow. Bellyful "arrives in camp with moose meat and bear meat, trade with sugar and tea.... Crossed river with Indian and saw grizzly bear tracks along beach." Milligan began building another cache for his supplies.

On October 21 Hart returned, to remain with Milligan at the Sikanni Chief site for the remainder of the fall. The men spent much of the rest of October building a cabin and finishing the cache. They completed the cabin's roof on October 26. Fortunately the weather was warm with a chinook blowing for several days. Milligan also took time to make some observations for latitude and longitude, and compared times with Hart, whose watch differed by about 18 minutes from Milligan's two watches. The two explorers also compared barometers, which had almost identical readings, and tested the sextants. Bellyful visited their camp a few times along with an occasional visit from other Sekani. Milligan wrote in his diary on October 28, Bellyful "passes through camp on way to hunt lynx", and three days later he "returns from hunt with portion of bear". Milligan bartered with the Sekani for meat and clothing that he needed for winter, using the value of a skin (or fur) as a bartering unit. On November 4 "Indians bring meat and moccasins, also mitts for Hart for which I pay out 13 skins [worth of] tea and sugar." His diary entry for that day also lists the supplies that he put in their cache.

In mid November Bellyful "passes through camp with his tribe and trades moccasin quill work. Paid 3 skins tea and sugar on Hart ... [and] traded three traps for quill robe" (valuable for keeping warm in winter). On November 18 Bellyful "returns again, sells mitts to Carty, 3 skins tea." The Sikanni Chief River froze on November 20, and a week later Milligan finished his canoe.

On November 29 "3 Indians arrive about noon with 2 dog teams (4 dogs each) sent to us by [Ed] Heron, HB post at Nelson. Give Hart my Hamilton watch as his stopped yesterday and when taken apart was put completely out of commission by breaking off of one of the points." On the last day of the month Bellyful and Metacar (another Sekani man) "arrive in camp with moose meat and the other Indians return with him to his camp. Paid Belly 2

Bellyful in Fort Nelson in 1915. He holds a black fox pelt and wears a medal he received from T.W. Parsons, the police constable for the region. Much later, in the 1930s, Bellyful became chief of the Sekani band in the Klua Lakes area. T.W. Parsons photograph; BCA A-06007.

skins tea, 3 skins sugar, 2 skins flour. Indians return in PM. Put up about 500 pounds [227 kg] supplies for the Indians to freight to Fish Lake tomorrow."

In a letter to the surveyor general in January 1914 Milligan explained why he had not been able to do much surveying in the fall.

> We had hoped to have carried the survey down river in November, but were disappointed in this, as the dog teams did not arrive from Fort Nelson till 19th December, which left us little time to get to the post before the mail left. Although the river froze over about the 20th November it was not fit for travel till late in December owing to the effect of chinook winds.

Mild weather continued into early December, as Milligan recorded in his diary on the first day of the month: "strong warm chinook wind all PM. Thermometer 46°F [8°C] and rising". On December 3 he "took photos of Sikanni valley showing bare hills and trees cleared of snow by recent mild

The Sikanni Chief River valley after a chinook in early December. LTSA.

weather." On December 9: "Snow all off the trees, the great depth of snow (about 12 inches [30 cm]) is attained in places sheltered from the wind." The next day the weather changed:

> The chinook wind stopped blowing about 4 PM and thermometer dropped steadily ever since with barometer rising. A halo was noticed around the moon this evening. All exposed hills have been cleared of snow during the winds of the last few days – and in places along the lower timbered flats not only was the snow all melted off in patches but ground was thawed and became muddy in places.

Milligan used the time to complete his paperwork and prepare for the trip to Fort Nelson. On December 18 he "started out this morning with pack for Fish Lake intending to see the Indians re dog teams. But about 10 miles [16 km] out meet Heron, post manager, with four teams who have crossed my trail and took another trail. I follow their tracks back and arrive at Sikanni Chief in evening. Pack up for early start in morning."

On December 19 Milligan, Hart and Cartwright started their 160-kilometre trip by dogsled to Fort Nelson. "Finally get away with five toboggan loads at noon – camp about 4 miles [6 km] along trail from top plateau. The country passed through is all burnt over, standing dead stick with second growth poplar, willow, alder and spruce with considerable marshy muskegs." The next day they departed at 6:30.

> Travel till 9:35 and feed at stream 1 chain [20 m] wide which we afterward follow down for about 3 miles [5 km]. We once more take to the brush and camp again, at 12:30 start again, and at 3 camp for the night.

Some of the dog teams that transported the men and their supplies to Fort Nelson. LTSA.

Beyond a few scattered clumps of scattered spruce along the creek bottoms nothing was noticed worth recording. 50% of the country is spruce muskeg.… In the timbered parts the ground is entirely bare and hard pulling for the dog teams.

They reached Fish Lake at 10 AM the next morning. "After taking on fish there we leave again at 1 and camp again at 4.... Del, the Sikanie chief at Fish Lake [is] a fine type of Indian." On December 22 they travelled all day, from 6 AM until 6 PM. Milligan wrote in his journal: "Very cold north wind – travelling not pleasant – 75% of country [we] pass through is muskeg." They arrived in Fort Nelson on December 23.

Left camp this morning at 8 AM, travelled till 11 and made fire, country passed through being principally poplar, willow, alder, second-growth spruce and pine with patches of muskeg. This good country continued till we reached the Nelson River when occasional muskegs occurred, and as we descended to the lower river flats the timber became larger. We followed the river down for about 10 miles [16 km] to Fort Nelson and on the flats on either side was excellent spruce timber. We arrived at the Fort about 4 PM.

Milligan, Hart and Cartwright moved into one of the Hudson's Bay Company's cabins. Fort Nelson would be their winter residence.

Meanwhile, in Victoria, Milligan's and Hart's explorations kept Surveyor General Dawson busy paying their expenses and dealing with more difficulties related to Hart. In late October Dawson received a letter forwarded to him by Dr Henry Young, the MLA for Atlin and northern BC. Dr Young

Stopping for a rest. LTSA.

had got the letter from W. Scott Simpson, the Indian Agent for the Stikine Division, who had received it, dated August 20, from Dick McDames.

Dear Sir,

Last summer a year ago I was working for Mr E.B. Hart with my two head of horses for 67½ days at $5.00 per day. Now Mr Hart issued me a cheque on the Canadian Bank of Commerce through Hyland and Belfry of this place. They forwarded same cheque to their bank for payment, and said cheque was returned to them, so of course I have not received anything in way of a settlement so far. Now I wish that you would take this matter up for me and do whatever you think best for go get a settlement for me. As Mr Hart is in the employ of the BC government you might be able to take action against him and collect the amount. Mr Hyland will advise you as to the cheque.

As I am getting old and not as strong as I used to be I wish you would do the best you can for me in this matter, so thanking you in advance for your attention in this matter.

I remain,

Indian Dick McDames

At about the same time Dawson received a letter from John Hyland of the Hyland and Belfry Store in Telegraph Creek.

Am enclosing a cheque of E.B. Hart's for $50.00. We understand he is going through this country on business for your department. This check was sent up from our interior post, there is no use in sending it to the bank, as all of his checks that we sent out have been returned, marked no funds. He has issued checks for almost $600 that are no good. Will you kindly let us know if these can be collected. Have had the Indian Agent here write Dr Young about one check he gave an Indian for work and horse hire, it was returned to us from the bank. If this check can be collected will you kindly have proceeds paid into our account, Hyland & Belfry, Royal Bank of Canada, Victoria, BC and if it is no good please return check to us and oblige.

The two personal cheques that Hart had made out to Hyland and Belfry in the spring for $337 and $50, probably for debts incurred in 1912, had proved worthless. The surveyor general sent a curt reply to Hyland on November 4.

Mr Hart is employed by this department in an exploration of the northeastern portion of this province and it would appear that while passing through Hazelton, he issued this cheque. The department assumes no responsibility for such cheques unless it can be clearly shown that they are for supplies or services rendered in connection with government work and information in this connection was not furnished by you.

In view, however, of the insufficient mail service between Telegraph Creek and Victoria, your request that this cheque be deposited to your credit was complied with, the cheque being duly accepted on presentation at the bank.

Under the above circumstances it is unnecessary to comment on your remarks to the effect that Mr Hart has issued a number of worthless cheques in northern British Columbia.

The following day he wrote to Simpson, reminding him that Hart's employment with the provincial government only started in the spring of 1913. "In view of the fact that the cheque was issued prior to Mr Hart's employment by this department, no action can be taken in this matter." But Dawson added: "The department are aware that Mr Hart has an account in the Canadian Bank of Commerce, Victoria, and are from time-to-time depositing to his credit money on account of salary."

He then wrote to Hart, summarizing his actions:

Your report dated 13th August, together with plan and letter reached this office on the 13th October and, in regard to the articles asked for, every attempt has been made to supply you with same as explained in my letter of even date.

In the matter of your expenses, the Department has paid accounts slightly in excess of $1000 and has also paid into your account at the Bank of Commerce $675.00.

In this connection I may say that a cheque for $50.00 drawn by you on the Canadian Bank of Commerce in favour of Messrs Hyland & Belfry was sent by them to this Department with the request that the money be deposited to their credit and this has been done.

There would also appear to be outstanding a cheque for $337.50, issued by you and payable to Indian Dick McDames. I have no knowledge that this cheque has yet been presented although the Indian Agent has written in connection with same.

These matters are brought to your attention in case the existence of these cheques should have escaped your memory.

I regret that I have been unable to obtain permission for you to shoot a wood buffalo.

The remittance of $40.00 to the Royal Geographical Society, mentioned in your letter, has been attended to.

I trust that you will continue to have the same good luck which you appear to have had to date and that you will be able to furnish me with reports of your progress from time to time.

Dawson sent a second letter to Hart regarding the explorer's list of requests made in August, informing him that he placed the order in November. "I have since heard from the Manager of the Hudson's Bay Co. stating that he will endeavour to have same shipped north as soon as possible."

The surveyor general also had to handle the information that Milligan and Hart were sending to him. After receiving Milligan's first report, sent in October, Dawson wrote:

I ... am extremely disappointed that your general opinion of the country is not higher than it is. However, it is distinctly your duty to report on the facts as you find them, and if the country is no good, the sooner this department knows it the better.... I want to impress it upon you that you gather all possible information in regard to the country in which you are working, as attention seems to be directed that way, and the department are withholding information in their possession until they get an authentic report from you.

The government had considerable interest in the resources of the region, particularly the agricultural potential, so the surveyor general would wait until Milligan and Hart completed their explorations in 1914 and submitted their complete reports.

Winter 1914

Immediately after arriving at Fort Nelson on December 23, Milligan, Hart and Cartwright began preparing for winter in northern BC. They first took up residence in a Hudson's Bay Company cabin at the post. There was no time to prepare for Christmas celebrations and Milligan's diary entry for the day said simply, "Christmas Day. Did nothing in particular." Between Christmas and New Year's Day some First Nations people arrived at the post, and Milligan asked them about the geography of the area east and south of Fort Nelson, which he intended to survey in 1914. On December 30 he wrote:

> Two Indians arrive from country to the east, also 4 Sikannis from country
> west of Fantasque [Fontas] River. Obtain useful information from these
> Indians in regard to their country. From Matsula, who hunts up Fantasque,
> I learn that canoes could be taken up his river and by a short portage one
> could reach headwaters of Hay River. None of the Indians know anything
> in regard to the three small upper Hay Lakes shown on the map. He also
> says that his country is all muskeg.

During the Klondike gold rush some of the people who took the overland route from Edmonton to Dawson City in the Yukon came through the Hay River drainage to Fort Nelson. Milligan was particularly interested in locating the route they travelled. Almost all of the Hay was in Alberta, but a small portion of the upper section of the river traversed through northeastern BC. He wanted to survey some of this portion in 1914, because it was the only area of his survey not in the North Pine or Fort Nelson drainages and its geography was virtually unknown to non-native people.

On December 31 Milligan wrote: "Two or 3 more Indians arrive in today – the last of those that are expected in." That evening he commented, "The Indians make the night hideous by continual firing of rifle shots." New Year's Day was a "beautifully clear day. Hold Indian dog races on river."

Fort Nelson, looking downstream. LTSA.

In 1913 Milligan, Hart and Cartwright had met only a few indigenous people of the area. In September Milligan and Cartwright had encountered one Dunne-za group in their territory north of Fort St John, and they'd had some dealings with Sekani people from the Klua Lake area in the fall. Hart had employed a few guides but had met no other First Peoples in his travels.

The First Nations people who lived in northeastern BC still mainly followed their traditional lifestyle. In their reports, all three commented on the attitude of these people toward non-natives. Milligan said:

> As the Fort Nelson region is away from the main line of travel, the only white men seen are those connected with the Hudson Bay Company, the Indian Agent, once a year, and the Roman Catholic missionary. The Indians have seen little of white people or civilized life, and consequently retain more of their original habits and customs than usually found among Indians nearer the border of civilization. There is difficulty in obtaining these Indians as guides or even in employing them in any capacity, and when one is engaged it is generally understood that in addition to his wages provision has to be made for his family. Once their confidence is gained, however, and a bargain struck, they are invariably found willing and honest.

Hart commented:

> The difficulties of travel in this section are increased by the unwillingness of the Indians to travel with or work for white men, and the scarcity of game, which makes the feeding of one's dogs whilst travelling a very serious question.

Dog-team races on New Year's Day on the Fort Nelson River. LTSA.

The Indians perhaps are hardly to be blamed, as these tribes, the Slavey and the Sikanni, have had no experience of white men and there is not one amongst them with a word of any language but his own. Consequently he finds no pleasure in white man's company, and if with great difficulty one is secured for a trip, it is always necessary to take a second one to keep him company.

And Cartwright said:

There are no Indian villages in the whole of the country covered. The tribes encountered were the Beavers [Dunne-za], who trade into Fort St John, and further north, the Sikanni and Slavey [Dene-thah] tribes, which trade into Fort Nelson. These tribes are nomad, and all three have their own language; however a few in each tribe have a small vocabulary of English. The Beavers, who hunt as far north as the Nelson River, are the only tribe possessing horses, consequently most of their trails are available for a pack train. Beyond the Nelson River, in the country of the Sikanni and Slavey, the trails are unfitted for horse pack trains.

From the foregoing, it will be noted that back packing is necessary over about two-thirds of this territory, except during the winter, when dogs and toboggans are used....

During the first season, the Indians were found to be very diffident in assisting with information on the country. However, their confidence was gradually gained, and eventually showed their willingness to help in the furtherance of the work.

Dene-thah camp at Fort Nelson. Photographer unknown; BCA A-06008.

As these Indian tribes rely upon hunting for the food, eating but little of the staple food the stores supply, they are not, in consequence available for hiring, their families being dependent upon them to keep the pot supplied with moose meat. They are good hunters. Their country is prolific in fur bearing animals.

During 1914 Milligan had more interaction with First Nations people, beginning in the winter when he took a few trips with the Dene-thah through some of their territory east of Fort Nelson, while Hart visited the Sekani in the Prophet River area.

Ed Heron, the Hudson's Bay factor at Fort Nelson, was preparing to take a trip downriver to Fort Liard. This was an opportunity for Milligan and Hart to send out reports, pictures and other material from their fall work, so both men spent the first days of January preparing their packages for the surveyor general. In Hart's letter to Dawson that accompanied his report he wrote:

I have just completed my report to you, such as it is, after much agony, and Milligan is still sweating over his. It's exceptionally difficult this time because neither of us has been able to do what we had hoped. I had expected to have been up to the head of the Prophet River and back before this, but the Indian whom I had engaged to put up meat for dog feed etc. went back on me and I was unable to do it. As you know, I ran across Milligan in his camp, whilst going over the country between the Sikanni (Chief) and the Prophet, and remained with him until we were able to get down on the ice. He has such an outfit that he must have a large amount of transport, whilst I, though not troubled with much of an outfit, have as much difficulty in moving in this part of the country because it is impossible to hunt and kill meat for my dogs. I shall be jolly glad when I get back into the mountains again where there is every kind of game.

After describing his proposed explorations for the winter Hart asked for more items he needed.

I've had to write to Wilkerson, Jeweller, in Victoria, asking him to send me up a good watch. I had a good one but it suddenly went out of action last fall and left me up against it. Without a good and reliable watch I can't hope to do work of much value, so I've given Wilkerson a limit of $200.00 and referred him to you. If he applies to you, would you mind arranging settlement with him?

I want some cross section paper, some Field Book size and some 10 x 12 sheets. And some tracing paper. Can you get me some? and a loose-leaf field book?

Milligan's report included some comments about the weather and his methods for gathering data about it:

It was found difficult to take maximum temperature readings when travelling and none were obtained except for a few days when in camp at the beginning of the season. The maximum and minimum thermometer were unfortunately broken and the spare thermometer being only a minimum. Temperature readings at our winter camp on the Sikanni Chief River were taken in the morning and evening, also at 2 PM which is approximately the time of greatest temperature during the day.

The direction of the wind was obtained generally by noting the movement of the low clouds; as from narrow valleys and timbered flats it is found difficult to obtain an idea of the movements of the air over the open country.

The winter so far has been comparatively mild; the weather during the greater part of November and December being particularly fair.

At our temporary winter quarters on the Sikanni Chief River, latitude 58°, where we were camped till December 19th, the snow, which usually fell in the form of fine powder of separate ice crystals, attained a depth of 8 to 10 inches [20–25 cm]. This was considerably lowered at time, however, by chinook winds which prevailed during the latter part of November and beginning of December; and along exposed side hills in places the ground was bare during the middle of December. The depth of snow increased to 2½ feet [75 cm] as we came north to Fort Nelson, the chinook winds having been felt only very slightly at this point.

Milligan also reported that he had not been able to explore much of the area during the fall.

Since last reporting in October we have not travelled any extent of new country, the only trip of consequence being from winter camp on the

Setting a Lynx snare. BCA A-04249.

Sikanni Chief River north by way of Fish Lakes to Fort Nelson, a distance
by winter trail of approx. 100 miles [160 km]....

The overland trail from the Sikanni Chief River to Fort Nelson, after
crossing over several high ridges or spurs of the foothills, follows about
N15°W through undulating plateaux country a distance of about 40 miles
[64 km] to the valley of Jack-fish Creek where a considerable extent of
excellent poplar and willow land is found. A proper examination of this
stretch of country between Fort Nelson River and the foothills has not
yet been made but from what could be gathered in a hurried trip through
it was noticed that, although spruce and tamarac muskeg predominates,
every variety of country is found, apparently in stages of transition from
muskeg to good willow land, giving evidence to bear out the contention
that when once burnt off and become dry these muskegs would in time
become good cultivable land.

Like Cartwright, Milligan realized the role of fire in the ecology of the
region's muskegs.

He was uncertain how much area he would be able to visit during the
winter.

In regard to our plans for the future it is difficult to state with much
certainty as to what our movements will be. Owing to the shortage of
dog feed, and the difficulty of obtaining any help from the Indians, the
only people who know the country, an extended trip to the Black River
Country this winter is out of the question. The intention now is to take
advantage of ice travelling while it lasts and so as much river survey as
we can, as this, I take it, is our best and cheapest means of extending an

Noon fire on the trip down the Nelson River with mail. LTSA.

accurate base survey through the country such as this, where triangulation
is almost impossible.

Milligan informed the surveyor general that he had ordered some equipment for his surveying work.

In cutting down weight for next summer I have decided to use the sextant for astronomical work, and in this connection I have written to Mr
McGregor, from whom I got the sextant, to obtain if possible an artificial
horizon and forward by mail to Fort St John. I have also sent out for an
almanac, watch, max and min thermometer and several other articles that
it is important I should have early next spring and have arranged for a
man to leave Fort St John with mail on May 15th. He would come as far
as the North Pine where I have arranged to meet him from this end. I
would also be able to send mail out by him when he returns in June. In
order to arrive at Fort St John by May 15th mail should leave Victoria by
the first week in April.

On January 5, "Heron and his man leave at 6 AM with two dog teams
for Fort Liard. There are only very few Indians around the post now, only a
few of those who have cabins." Two days later the men moved to an unoc-
cupied cabin near the post "formerly occupied by free traders." They spent
most of the following week around the cabin and Milligan developed his
photographs.

On January 18 Milligan began his first survey trip from Fort Nelson,
leaving with Albert, a First Nations mans who was taking a dog team and

a load of dog feed to meet Heron coming back from Fort Liard. "Recent snows have filled the trail and travelling necessarily slow. Travelled about 11 miles [18 km] downstream and camped at 5 PM, dark…. Fresh signs of pack of wolves at one point along river." The next day, they made about 32 kilometres "breaking trail all the way with snowshoes. Passed Snake River (nah doh dezey) during morning…. In most places the timber confined to fiver flat, the slopes being generally second growth spruce, poplar and willow."

Along the way Milligan tried to make a traverse of the river, but had to give up because it "became so tortuous, necessitated stopping too often. The following day the men travelled another 30 kilometres downriver. After breakfast on January 21

> Albert started down Liard [with] dogs and empty sleigh. He was back
> again in less than an hour with Liard boy who had come from Fort Liard.
> We then started back up river, camping at cottonwood point. In a letter
> brought from Mr Heron I learn that he has gone down to Fort Simpson
> with the mail and will be back at Nelson February 10.

After a short night the group "left camp at 1 AM, travelled till 7 AM and stopped for mitsoo.★ Snowed all night. Travelled again from 8:30 till 1 PM and again from 2:30, arriving at Fort Nelson 7:30 PM – about 45 miles [72 km]."

Milligan recorded the lowest temperature that winter late January: -51°F [-46°C]. He remained in and around the cabin until February 6, when he "made a short trip … back from top of bench west of the post. Good view was obtained of country west of the river, also the Rockies could be seen behind the escarpment. I judged the snow to be at least 2 feet [60 cm] deep and in the hollows more where the snow had drifted." The next day Milligan went out and took some photographs from different viewpoints.

Ed Heron had still not returned by February 10, so some First Nations men took three dog teams downriver to break a trail for him. They returned in the evening having gone about 15 kilometres without meeting him. Two days later, Milligan retraced their trail and found it covered in fresh snow.

By mid February the people in Fort Nelson began to run short of food. In Hart's report, he stated, "It was necessary to conserve our small supply of provisions for the spring, [so] we were compelled to spend a greater part of our time setting rabbit snares and attending to them in order to obtain rabbits for both ourselves and the dogs to live upon."

Milligan's diary entry for February 16 describes the severity of the food shortage:

> Making rabbit snares. Since we arrived at this point last Christmas it has
> been brought home to us very forcibly that before spring there will be a

---

★ *Mitsoo* is a Cree word for food. In winter, a stop for mitsoo usually included making a fire to boil water for tea to drink with your food.

severe shortage of grub of any sort. I have put aside enough together with our cache at Sikanni that I think should be sufficient to do us until the H.B. transport's arrival of next summer.

At the present time the H.B. Co. could not supply us with anything in the way of grub. We haven't used flour for the last 10 days – which however has been no great hardship as we have been fortunate in obtaining potatoes [purchased these from a First Nations person who grew them at Fort Nelson]. What flour we have is being kept till we start travelling again.

We have decided to do a "big rabbit hunt" to obtain feed for Hart's dogs and also meat for ourselves.

The next day:

Hart and myself make trip 3 miles downriver this morning and start snare line. As we started on our return we were joined by Mr Heron and party (including R.C. Priest and Indian Tom) with 10 dogs from Fort Liard. They had had a very hard trip being 12 days travel from Liard and they started with only 7 days feed for the dogs and themselves. They were pretty well done up when they got here. The only news of the outside world useful was something about a wind on Lake Superior – not very exciting. I got three letters two private and remaining only from Fawcett, DLS, who with his party is wintering at Fort Simpson. Hart received mail, some from G.H. Dawson.

On February 20 he wrote, "practically all the Indians that have stayed around the post since New Year have taken to the stick [forest] on moose and rabbit hunt." Most of Milligan's diary entries for the rest of the month include a daily count of rabbits snared. One entry mentions an evening visit by Heron and Almire Bezannier to play cards. Bezannier, the Catholic missionary priest for the Mackenzie River district, travelled south to Fort Nelson every winter.

At the end of February Milligan made observations for latitude and longitude for two days. The only known longitude for the post had been made by William Ogilvie, a Dominion Land Surveyor, in 1891. Milligan wanted to establish as precise a longitude as possible at Fort Nelson.

In March, as the days grew longer and the weather warmer, Milligan (with Cartwright's assistance) began surveying around Fort Nelson and established a survey station near the Hudson's Bay post. He realized that there were some open hillsides around Fort Nelson that he could use for a triangulation survey. In December, when he had come from his fall headquarters on the Sikanni Chief, he did not have time to do any surveying. He planned to return to the Sikanni Chief in the spring and needed to connect his surveying around Fort Nelson with the work he had completed the previous summer. To the south he could see some of the foothills of the Rocky

Fort Nelson, looking upstream to where the Muskwa flows into the Fort Nelson River. Milligan used the open, snowy hills on the horizon to the left for his triangulation survey. RBCM PN03393a.

Mountains. A triangulation survey between Fort Nelson and the Sikanni Chief River along these hills would be the quickest and most accurate way to cover this area. This was the western edge of the territory that Milligan was covering in his exploration and the only part that had hilly terrain. It would be his only opportunity to use triangulation surveying and to connect distinctive features of the landscape from multiple locations.

Milligan needed to have a distance and two angles to begin his triangulation survey. To do this he had to establish two surveying stations on hills near Fort Nelson and measure a baseline. Initially he examined the nearby river benches, but he could not find places that gave him an open view to the foothills to the south. On March 7 he found a suitable hill about eight kilometres west of the post and set up a triangulation station there. Mindful of the shortage of food he set 11 rabbit snares on the way back, and when he checked them two days later he found six rabbits. That day, he and Cartwright established two more triangulation stations on a hill behind the fort and another two at the ends of the baseline along the Fort Nelson River. On March 10 they measured the distance of the baseline and the angles from the triangulation stations. From these stations, Milligan read angles with his theodolite to the higher hill eight kilometres to the west. At this western station, he could see the surrounding countryside for many kilometres, especially in the south and west, where he wanted to make a triangulation survey on the way back to the Sikanni Chief River. Milligan had set up and started the triangulation survey that he would use during the first part of the spring.

Tom and his wife at Fort Nelson. LTSA.

That day the First Nations hunter, Matsula, arrived in Fort Nelson from the Fontas River area. Milligan arranged to see him the next day.

> Held wa-wa with Matsula in the afternoon and gained more informa-
> tion about his country. He tells me that it takes three days to cross the
> portage from the Muskwa to Hay Rivers. There are large cottonwoods
> on Hay River, however, out of which one can make dugout. He said
> when he used to make dugouts on the Hay River he used the blade of a
> plane to gouge out the log. Determined to see his country myself and to
> get supplies out to the portage by dog team, I completed arrangements
> with Heron this evening whereby if Cartwright would go down river the
> day after tomorrow with Tom and bring up cache of tin and quicksilver,
> he will, when they return, take a load of grub out to Matsula's camp on
> Fantasque River.

During the next two days Milligan expanded his triangulation network by surveying from several hills around Fort Nelson. "Take topo[graphic] notes of country from hill behind post. In the afternoon visit snare line and bring back eight rabbits." He completed his survey of the area on March 13 at a station he set up on a hill about six kilometres west of the post.

The next morning, Cartwright and Tom started downriver with a dog team. "They will bring tin and quicksilver at cache about 50 miles [80 km] from here." While Cartwright was gone Milligan spent a day developing photographs he and Hart had taken. "Am very pleased with results."

On March 16 he wrote in his diary: "Kidney Fat and Jesus, two Indians from Fish Lake way arrive with furs – also Matois and his boy from the country west of here. They are all catching plenty of lynx. The old Priest came in this evening with a hard luck yarn. He had been out all day on his snare line and brought back only one rabbit. 17 had been taken by wolves. Obtained lynx meat from Matois." The next evening a Dene-thah man arrived from Snake River and Milligan learned more about Hay Lake country from him. Cartwright and Tom returned on March 18.

G.B. Milligan

On March 19, "a beautifully sunny day", Milligan departed on his first exploration of the area east of Fort Nelson.

> Left the fort this morning at 6:30 with Indian, back packing, travelled over to his camp northeasterly arriving at 7:30 PM having stopped an hour for noon – distance about 25 miles [40 km]. For the first half of the way the trail was fairly well beaten and we made good time. The rest of the way however we followed a snowshoe trail and my snowshoes being a trifle small I would be continually breaking through. My guide, who had an exceptionally large pair, could stride along with comparative ease over the faintly marked trail. At their camp they fed me lashing of moose and lynx meat.

The next day:

> I left the Indian camp this morning at 7:45 with old Siwash as guide.
> Made a trip to mouth of Komie River and returned to Indian camp at 10.
> I found nothing very interesting this morning. Bear Track Creek [today Sahtaneh River] 150 links [30 m] wide, lies in a narrow valley. I left the Indian camp with my pack at 1 PM and struck back for Fort Nelson. I travelled 3½ hours and made camp.... I can generalize in a few words by saying that the country rises gradually from valley of Bear Track Creek and is timbered with 6" [15 cm] poplar and spruce, while from where the country starts to slope to the south it has been at one time burnt, there being now second-growth poplar and willow with dead stick windfall, also large stretches of scrub spruce and tamarac, muskeg in places fairly open.

On March 21 Milligan returned to Fort Nelson. "I left the camp this morning at 6:30 and arrived back at Fort Nelson at 5 PM after long stop for noon near Snake River making an estimate distance of 30 miles [50 km] from the Fort to the Indian camp.... Mild in the afternoon. Snow melts and causes heavy going with long snowshoes."

As soon as he returned he made arrangements for a trip to Fontas River. "Interpreter Peter with five dogs will take load of supplies to Matsula's camp." A blizzard kept Milligan at Fort Nelson all the next day, but March 24 was a "bright clear day with cold north wind. Left Fort Nelson this morning at 9 AM with Peter and five-dog team laden with about 175 lbs [80 kg] supplies for Fontas River. Recent storms had more or less drifted up the trail and the going was heavy. When we stopped and made camp for the night I figured we made about 17 miles [29 km]. A route survey is being made and topo[graphy] notes taken as we go along." They travelled all of the next day, covering about 40 kilometres, mostly over level muskeg.

Peter, an interpreter for the Hudson's Bay Company. BCA H-00480.

March 26 was another clear day.

> The north wind counteracted any affect the bright sun had on the snow and being very dry the travelling was excellent. For the first part of the day we continued through the almost limitless muskeg and after passing a small lake we commenced to gradually descend apparently being on the watershed of Fantasque River. On the down slope the country improved and patches of spruce, poplar and willows were frequently met. We camped for the night at 6 PM having come an estimated distance of 27 miles [43 km].

With the clear sky Milligan made an observation on the star Procyon for latitude that evening.

Good weather continued the next day. In his diary Milligan described meeting a group of Dene-thah:

> We got away from the camp at 6:30 this morning, and after travelling about an hour and half we came to forks of the trail with well beaten and fresh sleigh tracks. While we were debating which one to follow we heard dogs barking, and taking the left hand trail we soon arrived at Fantasque's camp.
>
> We found only the women and children at home, the men having gone off on a meat hunt. A runner was sent after the chief, Matsula, who arrived back late in the evening. We got the usual story of starvation, but managed to obtain a little dried moose meat for ourselves and dogs. Matsula, at first, did not seem inclined to do very much for us, but being very

Dene-thah camp. RBCM LS 369a.

The confluence of the Fontas and Kahntah rivers, an important location in Milligan's surveying network. He returned there a couple of times during his summer surveying. LTSA.

Looking down the Fontas River in winter. LTSA.

short of tea himself, it was by parting with ½ of my supply that he was finally induced to take us tomorrow to a point near the Hay Lake portage where we will cache our supplies.

I also obtained from him all the information that I could regarding his country viz names of streams, etc. Then, after noon, I made a trip down to the banks of Fantasque River distant about 3½ miles [6 km] from the Indian camp. The country noted generally and couple of photos taken of the valley.

With Matsula's assistance Milligan reached his objective the next day.

We got away from the camp shortly after sunrise and following a well beaten Indian trail for about 14 miles [23 km] we arrived at the cache at junction of Fantasque and Kahntah Rivers in time to obtain meridian altitude of the sun for latitude. Information was obtained regarding the portage that will help us when we come up by canoe. After safely caching the grub in Indian log cache we started back and arrived at the Indian camp at 6:30.

Milligan was ready to return to Fort Nelson on March 29. He had explored new country, almost reached the Hay River drainage, cached supplies for his return in the summer and established latitude at an important location of his route survey. The clear sky had gone and by that evening snow began falling.

We obtained a little dried meat from the Indians this morning, enough for small load for the Post. We got away from the camp at about 7 having being joined by Indian "Two by Six" who is going into the Post for tea. The trail, returning, was in good shape for travel and we made about 33 miles [53 km].

Crossing the Snake River. LTSA.

From "Two by Six" I obtain names of all the creeks, etc., besides useful information about the country generally, all of which is entered in field notes of route survey on the map.

In his journal Milligan described their full day of travel on March 30. Snows practically all day with cold northeast wind.

We travelled from 7 in the morning till 7 at night stopping twice for 'mitsoo' and made camp within few miles of Snake River. During the day's travel we came from the slope of Fantasque River Valley on to the height of land and crossed miles and miles of muskeg. The growth on the muskegs generally scrub spruce in places mixed with tamarac, in places partly burnt and occasionally we crossed patches of practically open muskeg with only few standing dead stick.

It is a hopeless looking country and in my own opinion, at least, in its present state, 75% of it may be classed as strictly mossy lands. We crossed several small muskeg lakes, surrounded, to the water's edge, with scrub growth of spruce and tamarac. Owing to the uniform nature of this country no distant views could be obtained but several photos were taken showing the muskeg country travelled.

They reached Fort Nelson on the last day of March.

Snowed during the night and was still snowing with north wind when we left camp at 6:30 this morning and continued so till we arrived at the Post at 2 PM. The recent snow has made slow travelling, especially so in the open muskegs where the trail was drifted over and in places was difficult to follow even for Indian "Two by Six". Snake River where we crossed it today is about 30 feet [9 m] wide and its bed lies within 10 feet [3 m] of surrounding muskegs. On either side of the creek to a distance of probably 2 chains [40 m] the ground is dry and willows and poplars are growing, but beyond that, scrub spruce muskegs extend for miles. When we came within 10 miles [16 km] of the Nelson River the country improved and second growth small willows poplars and alders are growing where, as evidenced by occasional standing dead stumps and upturned roots, was once a growth of fairly good sized timber. The upturned roots also reveal a clayish soil.

When I arrived back at the post I learned that Hart had "pulled out" several days before with Indian Malcolm and his band from the country between the Prophet and Fish lakes. His idea being to travel with the Indians and return with them when they come in with canoes in May.

In a letter to the surveyor general in June, Milligan summarized the winter he spent at Fort Nelson.

The weather last winter generally speaking was mild and agreeable. The lowest temperature reading recorded was 51° below zero on the 25th of January. During the coldest weather in January and February the days were usually clear with 3 or 4 hours of bright sunshine. Most of the snow fell during the month of February; the average depth at Fort Nelson being about 3 feet [90 cm]. In March, with the exception of several slight blizzards, the weather was very fair, usually marked by bright sunshine.

Last March a trip was made northeast of Fort Nelson through the Snake River country and also another trip about 90 miles [145 km] SE to Fontas River where a cache of supplies was made for use this summer. During January and February it was found impossible to do very much owing to the depth of snow and the fact that the H.B. Co.'s dog teams were away on trip to Fort Simpson.

His letter also provided an overview of the area.

The country northeast of Fort Nelson may be described as a gentle undulating plateau with an elevation of approximately 1600 to 1800 feet [500–550 m] or about 400 feet [125 m] above the river. The several streams which drain the area viz Snake River Sahtaneh Creek and Komie Creek flow in shallow depressions which as they approach the Nelson become deeper and more sharply defined.

With the exception of occasional scrub timbered muskegs the greater proportion of the country south from Sahtaneh Creek has been burnt over, and the present conditions of standing dead stick and windfall give the appearance of great desolation, but comparatively little labour would be required to clear the land.

On the trip southeast to the junction of the Fontas and Kahntah rivers,

> the country passed through was found to be at least 50% moss covered with growth of scrub spruce and tamarac, the balance being strips of good land along the creeks and patches where the country had been burnt over. The country improves after leaving the partially drained upper plateau and descending to the valley of Fantasque River.

Of the area east of Fort Nelson,

> the striking feature is the absence of hills and the uniformity of the surface of the country. A trip was made through a portion of this district about latitude 57°50 and although a great proportion was found swampy some excellent stretches of poplar and willow land were encountered along the valley of Kahntah River. [The bench land above the river] is practically all good agricultural land about 75% being poplar and alder, the balance moss covered with standing dead stick.... All the country has a gentle slope to the north and drainage of these swamps would be a simple matter.

Milligan concluded by saying:

> The more we see of this country the more favourable is the impression as to its possibilities. Undoubtedly a large proportion of the country is moss covered. The percentage of bog or muskeg however is small and the term 'muskeg' in referring to the mossy areas is misleading and is to be deprecated. When the moss is removed good soil is invariably found, varying from black loam 2 inches to a foot deep to clay loam or occasional clay with sand.... Very little gravel or rock on the surface is found anywhere.

As April began spring started to arrive. On April 2 Milligan mentioned in his diary the wet snow that made travelling difficult "during the heat of the day". He planned to return to the place on the Sikanni Chief River where he had spent the fall and there meet Fred Hazen, who was supposed to bring in supplies. He made arrangements with Heron regarding a trip with their supplies as far as Fish Lake. On April 3, "Matois and Matsula arrived, having killed a couple of moose a day's travel from here. Mr Heron is sending his dog teams out to bring the meat in, and as soon as they return we will leave for the Sikanni." While he waited Milligan hiked "along Fantasque's trail" about 10 kilometres to complete his route survey and tie in "Little Lake". He also worked on his meteorological reports and other survey material. Tom and Peter returned late in the evening of April 8 and reported that travelling was very slow in the wet snow. The weather turned mild the next day so they were unable to travel.

Then on April 10 at about 4 AM, under a clear sky with a bright moon, Milligan and Cartwright left Fort Nelson with Tom and two dog teams. They were about to begin an eventful spring.

E.B. Hart

In his report to the surveyor general, E.B. Hart described his trip to visit a band of Sekani in the Prophet River watershed in March.

I had been endeavouring since last Fall to make some arrangement with the chief of the band of Indians who hunt on the Prophet River and up-per waters of the Musquah, and had from time to time been disappointed by them. Promises were apparently made only as affording the simplest way of putting me off for the time being, as I learn from other sources that they did not want white men in there at all.

However, early in March, when three of the band came in bringing me a message from the chief to the effect that he could not go anywhere with me at present, I told them that I was going back with them and that they would have to provide meat for me whilst I was with them.

They did their utmost to frighten me, telling me that it was useless to take a dog-team, of the difficulties of the country, and also that they were starving and that I might starve if I went. However, I took all this with a very large pinch of salt, and having put up some tea, sugar and tobacco, I left with them on snowshoes, leaving dogs behind and carrying pack.

During his 1913–14 explorations Hart acquired some clothing items from the First Nations people. He sent six items to the Museum of the American Indian in 1927, including this Dene-thah baby sling. It is made of moose hide, otter fur, velvet and sewn beadwork. Today this object is housed in the Smithsonian National Museum of the American Indian in Washington, DC. NMAI 15/4648.

He and the three Sekani men followed a route southwest across the plateau between the Fort Nelson and Prophet rivers, and when they reached the Prophet travelled on the ice for about 30 kilometres. They then headed slightly southwest away from the river and eventually rejoined the Prophet near its headwaters. From there they headed to the Besa River, a tributary of the Prophet.

> I found that a dog team would have been very useful in going out, but useless out there, as the snow was going too rapidly; that there were no special difficulties in getting about the country, but that their stories regarding starvation were most unpleasantly close to the truth. The band consists of over 50 – men, women and children, and of this number only 6 are able-bodied hunters, the rest being women and children. It was a poor game country, on the whole, and, as may be imagined, a moose would not go far amongst so many. My tea and sugar did not last very long, and for the greater part of the time my diet consisted of rabbits, cooked by the Indians and only those who have experienced Indian cooking know what this means – and cold water.
>
> Neither a strengthening nor fattening diet, and I lost 30 lbs [14 kg] on the trip, weighing only 120 lbs on my return, in place of 150 [68 kg]. However, it is only fair to state that when once I reached their camp, nothing could exceed the Indians' willingness to do all in their power for me. Whenever they had meat they took care that I should have plenty, and when I was laid up for three or four days with lumbago, they simply crammed me with horribly nasty messes – which I was of course compelled to swallow and say how good they were – but which perhaps proved the most efficacious means they could have devised for getting me on my feet again.

After leaving the band at the Prophet River, Hart headed west, "across and up the Prophet River, to the point at which it emerges from the Rocky Mountains". He described the area on the eastern side of the Rockies in the Fort Nelson area: "The whole of this country East of the Rockies appears to be a level plateau through which the rivers have cut comparatively narrow channels to a depth of from 200 to 300 feet [60–90 m]. The plateau is for the greater part wet, and moss-covered, and having a scrub growth of small spruce, pine, and, in some few places, tamarac." He realized the beneficial role of fire in the ecology of the area. "Where, however, fires have completely cleared the surface, the moss has dried up and there is a good growth of grass, proving the natural fertility of the soil if put under cultivation."

His exploration of the area led him to report:

> The Prophet and Musquah rivers issue from the Rockies in lat[itude] 57°47'22", one on either side of the same mountain. In fact, one branch of the Prophet heads in the mountain. The Prophet River runs slightly

Another of the items Hart sent to the Museum of the American Indian in 1927. This Sekani jacket is made of moose hide with fur and bird quills. It also now resides in the Smithsonian collection. NMAI 15/4649.

north of east for about 40 miles [65 km] before turning north and the Musquah runs first for 10 miles [15 km] north and then about N20°W until it takes its bend to the east near the Tetsa…. Lying between these two rivers, and also on the south bank of the Prophet River, there is in all about 200,000 acres [81,000 ha] of perfectly dry bench land, which has been almost entirely cleared of timber by fire and which supports a good growth of grass, and over which the Beaver Indians [Dunne-za] from Fort St John used formerly to range their horses when hunting in this locality.

Hart described Wahthinli Mountain and its significance to the First Peoples of the area:

The mountain which separates the Prophet and the Musquah Rivers is deserving of special mention…. It is not only remarkable as being the highest mountain in the range, for its altitude is probably not much over 8000 feet [2400 m], but for its remarkable appearance, and as being the subject of Indian legends and traditions. It is visible from a very long distance to the north and northeast. From the northeast it appears to be split straight down from the summit for about 2000 feet [600 m].

As the Indian tradition concerning it is that in former generation their god had a house on this mountain and constantly lived there until the annoyance caused by the number of animals which congregated on the mountain caused him to leave, I have ventured to call it The Mountain of the Gods. The summit is formed by two points like horns, approaching one another, at the present time some 600 feet [180 m] apart, but which the Indians say, at the time of the god's residence on the mountain were almost touching one another and have since his departure been gradually receding; and from these points, or horns, the mountain is split for 2,000 feet [600 m] sheer, out of the bottom of which gap a fork of the Prophet River runs.

In the letter sent with his report, Hart added: "Just as an instance of their adaptability and willingness to please, I might add that they say now that Jesus Christ lives there." Because Wahthinli was so important, Hart said he took the greatest care to obtain the position of the "Mountain of the Gods" and so to fix the position of the eastern boundary of the Rockies at this latitude, both by travel and by numerous compass bearings, and as the traverse of my route survey, when worked out on my return to Fort Nelson – although necessarily taken to only 5 degrees as it was hard to work closer from a moving canoe – placed me within 4/5 of a mile in latitude and practically correct in longitude, I think I may consider position of above mountain to be substantially correct.

[I] had intended taking differences of longitude, but found the cheap watch, which is the only one obtainable at present, too unreliable.

Hart remained in the upper Prophet River watershed well into spring.

Spring 1914

G.B. Milligan

With the First Nations man, Tom, George Milligan and William Cartwright headed their dog teams from Fort Nelson toward the Klua Lakes. They brought with them another dog, named Tomato, acquired to replace Prespa-tou, who had gone missing last August near the Blueberry River.

> We travelled up the river for about 11 miles [18 km] and then took to the winter trail making Dan's camp at Jackfish Creek at about 4 PM. Tom and Cartwright handled the dog teams and I was free to make route survey, etc. Up till about 9 in the morning the trail was fairly firm under foot and travelling was good, but the sun soon softened the snow and from the river to Dan's camp we made very slow time.... We camped at Dan's brush tipi and during the evening I observed Procyon for latitude.

Milligan climbed the hills above Jackfish Creek, where he had a good view of the area to the south and east and took some photographs. Perhaps because of the spring weather, he expressed a new optimism about the countryside. "The notes of the many spring birds, occasional bumblebees, butterflies, and frogs croaking in the ponds remind one that summer is at hand, and sweating with the heat, as I clambered down the hill back to camp it took very little effort of the imagination to predict a hopeful future for parts of this corner of the province."

That night the temperature dropped again.

> [It] froze the snow again and we made excellent time with the dogs for the first few hours after we left Jackfish Creek. We travelled till 6:30 in the evening and made about 24 miles [40 km]. The trail follows just east of the foothills, the country rising gradually as we went south. An indifferent sort of country, scrub spruce with moss predominating while we passed through occasional patches of second growth birch and willow.

Fish Lake country, looking east. BCA I-67821.

On April 12, their third day of travel, they reached the Klua Lakes.

Slight fall of snow last night. As usual we had a few hours of good travelling in the morning and for the rest of the time we laboured through the
wet snow at a rate of about 1½ miles an hour. There were several inches
of water on the ice on Fish Creek and it was necessary to lay down poles
for the toboggans to cross on. The snow is going very fast and in exposed
spots and in muskegs the ground is bare in patches.

They camped that night near the Hudson's Bay Company fish cache at the
lake and Milligan once more measured the stars to obtain latitude.

He and Cartwright spent a few days at the fish cache. The country around
the Klua Lakes had hills that enabled Milligan to continue the triangulation
surveying he had started at Fort Nelson and allowed him to see much of the
area that he was going to explore during the 1914 field season.

On their first day there it snowed until mid afternoon.

Tom took on a load of whitefish and started back for the post [Fort Nel-
son], Cartwright going back with him as far as Fish Creek. I spent the day
myself up till 3 PM climbing the hills to the south. It snowed after I got to
the top and I was unable to obtain any view. Travelling along the top of
the hill was very difficult through the tangle of alders and jack pine. I left
a station at each end of the hill and returned to camp by way of the summer trail to the Sikanni.

On April 14, while the weather was clear and Cartwright gone for the
day, Milligan went back along the trail towards Fort Nelson and climbed a
hill on the north side of Fish Creek. "I had taken azimuth bearing of this
hill from my station near Fort Nelson. A splendid view of the country in
every direction was obtained from this point and angles were taken with
the light transit to all prominent features as lakes, hills, creeks, etc." Now he

was able to survey back to his station with a flag near Fort Nelson, extend his triangulation surveying south to the Klua Lakes and connect it with the features that he could measure around the area.

> I also took three photos, one of a portion of the Rockies behind the foot hills. I left camp at 7 AM and returned in the evening at 6:30. The photos taken would also show the uniform nature of the country to the east, especially east of the Nelson River. Between the foot hills and the river the country is almost level and the growth appeared all 2nd growth.... Numerous marshy lakes were dotted here and there. Observed for azimuth and LMT [local meridian time].

The weather was mild that night and the temperature did not get below freezing. Since the snow was wet, Milligan and Cartwright spent the next day setting up a baseline at Klua Lake, like they had done along the Fort Nelson River, running it across the lake from the camp. They measured the distance using a stadia rod and his theodolite (which had two horizontal cross hairs called stadia hairs in its viewing scope). This method enabled Milligan to obtain a distance quickly and with only two people; although not as accurate as using a surveying chain, it still provided a high degree of precision. From each end of his baseline he measured an angle to his station on the hill. With two angles and a distance he was able to make a triangulation at the Klua Lakes and could then connect it to his station at Fort Nelson.

In the afternoon Milligan "worked out astronomical observations, etc., to date. We were fortunate in obtaining about 40 whitefish that were left in the cache here by the HBC. They are most delicious eating. Today Cartwright split and hung them up to dry in the sun."

On April 16 Milligan and Cartwright began moving their supplies and equipment from the Klua Lakes to their fall camp on the Sikanni Chief River. They would have to make some relay camps along the way. The temperature had dropped below freezing the night before, which made moving their goods much easier. "With hand sleigh we moved our camp and outfit to the south end of the lake. We made two trips and got camp up at noon and in the afternoon packed a load each, ahead a few miles."

The next day Milligan returned to surveying.

> It cleared yesterday evening after the sleet storm and this morning was bright sunshine while in the afternoon it clouded over at intervals.
>
> Cartwright took the toboggan back to the cache this morning and in the afternoon packed a load (himself and dog [Tomato]) ahead 3 miles [5 km]. I completed topographical sketches and transit angles from hill 4 in the morning and [hill] 3 in the afternoon and also packed a load along the trail to top of first hill from camp.
>
> From hill 4 I took photo looking towards Fish Lake.

From hill 3 a splendid view was obtained of the country to the east and I was able to sketch in the lake and courses of the creeks between the foothills and the Nelson River. The striking feature of the entire region to the east of the foothills is the uniformity of its surface. Easterly from the Nelson River the country rises very gradually to the plateau and height of land between the drainage areas of the Nelson and Hay rivers and which representing my horizon presented a straight unbroken line.

A growth of spruce timber usually followed the courses of creeks, the balance of the country being covered by 2nd growth jack pine, willows with also a large percentage of marsh and scrub spruce muskeg.

Milligan completed his survey in the Klua Lakes area on April 17, so the next day he and Cartwright continued moving their gear toward the Sikanni Chief River.

We packed our camp outfit past our relay cache made a few days before. We followed the summer trail for part of the way but afterward got off on a branch trail that took us westerly to the winter trail at the junction of which we made camp. Although the snow is fast going there is still enough in patches to make travelling laborious. Passed through an indifferent country being more scrub spruce and tamarac than anything else.

On April 20 Milligan wrote in his diary: "What little snow there is left is soft and travelling is very slow. De ha cho Creek is open and we had to throw a tree across." But the next day,

the trail was hard in the early morning owing to last night's frost but became very sloppy in the afternoon. After crossing De-ha-cho Creek and ascending the bench on the south side we found ourselves on a fairly dry plateau…. From a view obtained from a high ridge, which we ascended after crossing the plateau, the country to the east and north appeared to be of a similar character, all 2nd growth with exception of fringe of spruce timber along the lower flats of De ha cho Creek.

Milligan could also see the Sikanni Chief River valley to the south.

They camped that night by a small lake where Milligan "heard grouse drumming for the first time this spring." They spent April 22 at their camp.

We went back this morning and packed balance of ictus [supplies] from the cache and in the afternoon Cartwright takes a load ahead towards Sikanni. I spent the afternoon with the transit on the hills and was able to get back bearings to Fish Lake hill, also angles up and down the Sikanni valley. A bush fire could be seen about 10 miles [15 km] down the river, evidently the Sikanni Chief and his band.

Milligan was able to extend his triangulation surveying from Klua Lakes to this location and continue it farther south to the Sikanni Chief River valley. Unfortunately it was cloudy in the evening so he was unable to make any observations on the stars.

The next morning he measured another baseline and did some triangulation surveys to hills on south side of Sikanni Chief River valley.

> In the afternoon we moved our camp on to the river and camped with the Sikanni Chief and his band whom we found encamped on the north side of the river, being engaged in making their bark canoe for the trip down river to Nelson. In travelling from our camp at the little lake to the bench at the Sikanni we traversed an almost level plateau, the greater part of which was muskeg, in places very boggy and wet with scrub spruce and tamarac. As we neared the Sikanni the country became drier and the growth varied from second growth spruce and poplar to black pine and poplar with occasional patches of burnt dead stick. Everywhere the soil which is light clayish is covered with moss varying from an inch to a foot in depth. Noticed geese flying north. Mosquitos bothered us this PM.

The surveyors had returned to the vicinity of their fall quarters on the Sikanni Chief River and met the Sekani again. Along the route, Milligan had been able to do some important triangulation surveying and mapping for his exploration.

On April 24, their first day back at the Sikanni Chief River, Milligan "sent Indians Ha ho and Det-sedah back to the little lake for balance of our outfit". When they returned in the evening "I paid them in sugar and cartridges." Bellyful had made a spruce-bark canoe that morning and used it to take Milligan, Cartwright and some of their equipment across the river.

Making a spruce-bark canoe. RBCM PN03240.

Paddling a spruce-bark canoe. RBCM PN03377c.

In his government report Milligan described the process of making a bark canoe.

> In the spring and summer, when they wish to travel downstream to the post they usually go by canoe. Being unable to secure birch bark in large enough pieces, their canoes are made of spruce bark.... They are very small and frail and seldom carry more than one man and his hunting outfit. They are used only for one trip and that downstream, and being so fragile are seldom taken upstream. They are convenient, however, as two Indians can make one in half a day. After selecting a suitable tree it is cut down and the bark peeled off in one piece the required length of the canoe. This is fitted and sewn on to a frame of spruce, the ends are sewn together, and the whole thing is ribbed with young willows and spruce.
>
> The knot holes are then gummed and the canoe is ready for the water.

After Milligan and Cartwright found that their cache made last fall was intact they set up camp about a kilometre downstream.

The next day Milligan began construction of his own water craft, a dugout canoe that would take four days to complete. "Picked out a suitable cottonwood tree close to camp and started at work making a dugout. The canoe I made last fall, it was decided, was too big for two men to handle going upstream. Cartwright made rabbit snares this morning and in the afternoon set them along the trail to St John."

On April 27:

> Bellyful and his band started down river this afternoon and part of the
> time was taken up with him and the balance of the day was put in on the
> canoe. I got him to take the big instrument [the theodolite] and Cart-
> wright's dunnage down to Ft Nelson. He promised to supply us with
> dried meat this summer at the post and I also obtained sketches from him
> of the Sikanni Chief River above this point.

The next day, "it took us a good part of the day to move the canoe down
to the water. It was found to be very 'cranky' and requires spreading." On
April 29 "W.H.C. [Cartwright] goes on a rabbit hunt and brings back six. I
finish digging out canoe ready for steaming and spreading."

Milligan described the last day of April as "a hard luck day":

> We split our canoe this morning when stretching it. It split from the stern
> to amidships and being impossible to repair I started out to the woods
> again to make another. The first tree I cut down after being barked was
> found to be badly twisted, so another one was felled and which with care
> I think should make a good canoe as it is fairly straight and the wood
> seems sound enough.

Milligan began May trying again to make another canoe. "W.H.C. on his
rabbit hunt runs across a cow moose but he had only the 22!!! [I] pounded
on the canoe all day. The wood is much tougher than the last one and the
log is much more difficult to hollow out."

He finished it on May 4. "Beautiful sunny day. After skidding the canoe
this morning from the woods to the beach we steamed and stretched her
and when afterwards tried in the water she rode right side up not only to
the satisfaction but also surprise of the builders. Made paddle this evening."

Now Milligan could resume his surveying:

> Made a trip today to top of hill northeast of camp and obtained compass
> bearings to trig points and Fort Nelson to Sikanni River survey, also topo-
> graphical sketches. The balance of the day was taken up with the canoe,
> finishing off the bow and stern, also setting in permanent cross pieces.
> W.H.C. hunts rabbits and obtained two and a chicken.

On May 6 Milligan set up a baseline and began a triangulation survey
along the Sikanni Chief River.

> Worked out observations this morning while the balance of the day was
> taken up with baseline along the river bar. From each end of the base,
> which was ¾ mile long, angles were taken to the high hills on either side
> of the river valley, the idea being to carry a system of rough triangulation
> on the trip upstream and also downstream as far as the hills will permit.

He had been unable to do any triangulation surveying of this area in the fall
of 1913, so he intended this spring to do as much as possible along the western edge of his exploration in the foothills of the Rockies. He could then

connect it to his 1913 survey, which he had tied to survey posts in the area around the north boundary of the Peace River Block. This, along with his observations on the sun and the stars, would make his surveying as accurate as possible for the amount of territory he covered with only one person to assist him. From these hills Milligan could survey any noticeable features to the east. By surveying these features from different stations on his way south he would be able to map them better.

In his journal he described his surveying on May 7:

> Left camp this morning at 6:30 taking with me the small transit, barometer and Kodak, etc., and climbed the hill south of camp, upon which was to be one of the angles of the initial triangle.
>
> I followed the horse trail for about a mile and a half and then branched off along the side hill on an Indian foot path that suited my direction as far as the top of the main bench when I took off across the flat south to the hill, reaching the top at 9:30....
>
> The hill, like all the others that I have climbed since leaving Fort Nelson, is capped with a rimrock of sandstone or a mixture of sandstone and (to use my own term) "pebble stone", which is really beach gravel that had been compacted together in solid masses.
>
> About two hours was spent on the hill and bearings taken to points up and down the Sikanni valley. I also obtained an azimuth to Fish Lake hill.

From this hill Milligan could survey all the way back to his first triangulation station south of Fort Nelson near the Klua Lakes. While there, he saw grass beginning to grow on the hills, and buds forming on the branches of the willows and birches.

The next day he plotted his surveys between Fort Nelson and his present location. He noted "Fort Nelson is moved 10 miles [16 km] to the east of its present position on the maps." The only previous attempt to establish the longitude for Fort Nelson was made by William Ogilvie during his 1891 survey for the federal government. Milligan's calculation was still more than a kilometre west of the actual longitude, but it was quite accurate considering his equipment and the imprecise time on his Blockley, which had not been corrected since he began surveying 10 months ago. He spent the next two days working on his map and doing office work, while Cartwright was "chasing rabbits".

On May 11 the two men headed up the Sikanni Chief River, where disaster struck:

> We left for upriver this morning with our canoe loaded somewhat heavily. Too big a load for the size of canoe.... We made fair time, however, till an unfortunate accident happened which almost put an end to our trip altogether. The canoe filled with water as we were heading her around a nasty windfall point. Everything of course was soaked. We had to dry the

stuff out and bale the canoe amongst the windfall and then reload her and cross the stream to the nearest place we could camp. When the ictus [supplies] was all spread out on the beach today and an inspection made of damage done it was found that the Kodak was out of order, all the stationary including finished tracing of work to date was ruined or practically so, and our grub – well it was soaked "mush and all and all in all". I suppose it might have been worse, however, for it was fortunate the whole outfit wasn't dumped and floated away.

They continued upstream the next day.

We seemed to have travelled a long way up stream today but I don't suppose we made many miles in a straight line from our camp this morning. The river follows a winding course between its benches and being at a very low (probably its lowest) stage the result is, there is barely enough water on the riffles and bars to float the canoe and a good deal of our time is spent in the middle of the stream lifting.... The valley is perceptibly narrowing and the high hills (foot hills) are closing in on either side.

On May 13 they canoed a few hours upstream, then camped close to the base of a hill. Milligan spent the afternoon surveying from the hilltop. The next day they continued upstream, camping at the foot of another hill.

Nothing unusual happened during the day except that I had my first bath since last fall. While poling up a nasty spot I lost my balance and tumbled out of sight in the river. When I got out I found much to my delight that although there was water inside the face of the watch, it was still going and is still going as I retire.

The river is becoming swifter and travel upstream more difficult, the trouble being that in the swiftest places there is generally not enough water to float the canoe and much delay is caused by having to practically drag the craft over the gravel and rock.

Fortunately, Milligan's half chronometer watch, vital for his survey work, survived the second accident on the river.

He spent May 15 surveying on a high hill above the Sikanni Chief River.

From camp this morning I crossed the river and mounted Hill 3 about 1200 feet [360 m] above the river. A good view was obtained for miles up and down the valley and angles were taken for topography, etc.

Looking across the river valley from my hill today I could see a long way up the valley of a fairly large stream which joins the Sikanni (from the southwest) about two miles below me. The valley appears as a wide gash in the rim rocked walls of the Sikanni valley and comes from the southwest, most likely from the glaciers of the Rockies.

On every side of me the country has been fire swept. In places as on the side hills opposite, the ground has been burnt of windfalls and grass is now growing affording excellent range country.

In most instances however the country needs another fire, as in its present state of windfall and alders it is almost impassable for man or beast.

The river flats have apparently not been touched by fires for they are covered with a growth of good sized spruce and cottonwood. In most instances however they have been flooded at high water and in places many feet deep as evidenced by marks on the trees.

Milligan also made an important discovery there:

On the top of the hill I found an Indian trail which I followed for some distance and found it bearing in a southwesterly direction and from the description given me by Indian Bellyful, I take it is the trail which joins with the trail to St John.... It is decided therefore that in view of the difficult upstream work with a heavy load to make a cache where this trail joins the river and then go on light for three or four days, probably as far as the canyon, and then return and go overland to meet our man from St John on the 25th of this month.

He and Cartwright resumed their trip up the Sikanni Chief River the next day: "The current being swifter than ever and the river winding, we did not make many miles in latitude. About 2 miles above camp, we made a cache at the point where the Indian trail comes to the river, the intention being to take this trail when we go overland to meet Hazen."

On May 17 they reached the canyon on the Sikanni Chief.

About 4 o'clock we camped at what I took to be the foot of the canyon as marked on the existing maps. Here the river is very winding and where it cut into the sides of its valley there are high steep cut banks. At its present low stage of water the river every ¼ to ½ mile tumbles over rapids in places with a drop I should estimate of two to four feet. At the canyon the river flows between low cut banks and at high water it would be almost impossible to take a canoe up it. As it is it would be most difficult for us to take our canoe through and we would risk losing what little stuff we have.

I cruise ahead above the canyon for a few miles and find that the river continues as swift as ever and decide it would be unwise to continue upstream any further. Where there are no cut banks the sides of the valley are covered with a growth of birch poplar, scrub spruce. There are small flats on the river with poplar or birch, and excellent alluvial soil, the greater part of these however would appear to flood at high water.

At the canyon Milligan found an old trail along the east side of the river and decided to follow it the next day.

It was a well cut out trail and I traced it for about eight miles [12 km], far enough I considered to be certain that from its direction, etc., it must connect with the trails to St John.

Shortly after I struck it at camp the trail crosses a couple of flats and then turns easterly and goes up the steep side of the valley and after reaches the top (1150 ft [345 m] above the river) it turns more to the southeast and passed through jack pine, spruce and poplar, with occasional muskeg, to the valley of a small stream that flows northwesterly (N40°W) into the Sikanni ... 3 miles [5 km] below camp....

I arrived back at camp at 3 PM and then started back downstream for the rest of our outfit (stationery and grub, etc.) it being decided that the trail I followed today was the one we should take to connect with our man from St John, and not the trail down river where we left a cache.

On May 19 Milligan and Cartwright went back to their camp down the Sikanni Chief River. "Two hours travel downstream today brought us to our cache and there we camped for the day. The trip was not without excitement as the current was swift, rapids occurring almost every few hundred yards, and in several of which we shipped water."

Before returning to the canyon Milligan did more surveying from a nearby hill. "This afternoon I cruised the country to west of River and from Hill No. 4 took transit angles to points up and down the valley. Tremendous fires have at one time swept this country, a good deal of which is now almost open with scattered charred logs and dead stick. This would make an excellent range country."

The next day the two men returned upstream, stopping for the night at an old First Nations camp on the west bank "where two or three trails come in from Prophet River country". This was an important campsite in the trail network of the area, a place where First Nations travellers built canoes to transfer from land to water. Milligan noted in his diary: "the Indians have made spruce bark canoes here, probably last summer", no doubt reflecting on his frustrations in trying construct a viable canoe.

On May 21 they arrived at the canyon trail, but along the way had one more disaster on the river. "Another nasty canoe accident – she nearly filled with water as she hung crosswise on a boulder in the middle of rapids. Our matches and tea kept dry, but practically everything else got wet." Milligan's dugout canoe had taken considerable time to make, yet could only be used for a short distance and its awkward handling had caused accidents that damaged valuable equipment (including his camera), notes and food.

Milligan and Cartwright started hiking the next day, intending to reach their cache on the North Pine in three days, where they would meet their packer, Fred Hazen.

Left camp at 7 this morning and followed the trail I had cruised the other day. The trail was fairly well marked in the green timber, evidently used by horses at one time, but when we got into the burnt country near the summit it was impossible to trace it further so that we continued up the creek keeping our own direction of south to southeast. It was estimated

we made about 15 miles [24 km] and camped at a point on the creek,
which I make by meridian altitude of Arcturus, to be in latitude of 57°35'.
Passed through practically all burnt country with dead stick and windfall.

They continued heading southeast the next day for about 15 kilometres.
The first part of the day was through muskeg (fairly dry), and patches of
pine and spruce with occasional thickets of 2nd growth pine and spruce,
all mossy ground. We had been gradually rising till about 9:30, five miles
[8 km] when we reached the top of green timbered hill which marks the
easterly boundary of the burnt country. For the rest of the day we were
scrambling through windfall and willows over rolling ridges that form part
of the summit between the Pine and Sikanni waters. In the burnt country
the grass is growing amongst the windfalls and should the windfalls and
dead stick be cleared off these summit hills would afford excellent summer
range for stock.

The next morning they reached the Nelson trail near their camp just
north of the divide between the Sikanni Chief and North Pine rivers. Since
he had followed a different route from the Sikanni Chief River to the summit than last September Milligan had completed another surveying loop.
This one included the triangulation survey that Milligan had done from the
hills above the river, which improved its accuracy.

From this camp the two men "went on a coal hunt up the headwaters of
Conroy Creek where I had seen coal last fall." Milligan "collected a handful of specimens and when I got back to camp put them on the fire. It was
found they burnt quite freely and left a sort of clinker." Milligan noted that
he was taking a couple small specimens to be sent out for identification.
Then the men continued south along the trail for a few hours before camping. For the first time this season Milligan noted, "Mosquitos ferocious."

May 25 was the day they were scheduled to meet Hazen. "Four hours
travel today brought us to the Treaty meadows, the point where we expected to meet Hazen from St John. We decided to camp here today and tomorrow, and if by that time Hazen didn't show up we would go on to the North
Pine. It was noted that the growth on the south side of the summit was not
so far advanced as on the Sikanni side." While waiting for Hazen the next
morning Milligan explored the country to the west. "Discovered Tredwell's
trail to the Sikanni and this I followed for about four miles [6 km]."

On May 27 Milligan and Cartwright continued south to the North Pine,
hoping to meet Hazen en route.

We shouldered our packs this morning and followed the Nelson trail back
14 miles [23 km] to the North Pine. It was not a happy couple that pitched
camp on the banks of the North Pine this evening. With Hazen three days
behind time we began to realize that something was wrong, either that
my letter sent from Nelson last winter had not reached him, or that some

accident had happened to Hazen. However, being out of grub, having left only tea, 4 square inches of bacon, 10 small biscuits and a handful of rice, something had to be done, and quickly. So after a little discussion it was decided that the only thing for us to do was to split up, Cartwright to hike into St John and myself to go back and travel what country I could till Cartwright returned with horses from St John. It was imperative that the St John trip be made as I required the photo films, almanac, watches, government letter, artificial horizon, and several other things I had sent for. It was therefore settled that Cartwright would make the round trip as quickly as possible and meet me towards the end of June at the Sikanni at the Nelson trail crossing. In the meantime I would explore the country easterly from Conroy and north of the summit and try to reach the headwaters of Notoza River. I would take the dog [Tomato] and travelling light should be able to cover considerable country in three weeks' time.

Hazen's failure to appear was a serious blow to Milligan's exploration. He needed food and supplies, but it was also important to make maximum use of the 1914 field season, and he did not want to take the time to go to Fort St John. He had confidence in both his and Cartwright's ability to travel through this wilderness. Milligan had a small amount of food, which he hoped to supplement by finding game animals. He had Tomato to carry supplies and for companionship, but he also had to feed him.

The next day:

We started in opposite directions this morning, Cartwright for St John and myself and Tomato back to the Sikanni. The North Pine being very low Carty waded without difficulty and continued with his pack consisting [of] 22 rifle, blanket, 6 biscuits, handful of tea, 2 inches of bacon, and handful of rice and an axe. He expected to reach St John in 5 or 6 days. My outfit consisted of a similar grub list, 30.30 rifle, sextant & mercury. I got back to Treaty meadow at 1 PM, having been fortunate in shooting two rabbits and a chicken. I turned down Tredwell's trail at 3:30 and travelled four or five miles [6–8 km], making route survey and topo notes and made camp by side of a small swamp creek. I noted robins for the first time since I left the Coast.

Milligan described his first day by himself.

I left camp at 7 this morning and at 4:30 I reached the trapper's cabin on the Sikanni ½ mile below which I made camp. A careful route survey was made from the Nelson trail to the Sikanni. From the summit I was fortunate in obtaining compass bearings both back to my starting point and forward down the valley of the stream I followed to the Sikanni.

For the first two miles from camp the country, which rises from valley to the summit, is nearly open, having been fire swept. There are scattered small jack pines and willows with dead stick. It was particularly noted that with the exception of a few places on the actual summit where there was green timber, the soil in the burnt second growth country both on the east and west slopes appeared to be excellent loose dark clayish loam with clay subsoil. Whether or not its altitude would be too great for agriculture, it would at least make excellent range country. Genuine muskeg is found in the patches of scrub spruce and tamarac. The moss is a couple of feet deep and wet. In my own humble opinion if the 2nd growth country which surrounds these islands of apparently worthless bog is the result of fires then I would say let there be more fires.

Some difficulty was had in tracing the trail through the burnt patches and at one creek, ½ mile from camp, it took me nearly an hour to pick up the trail on the other side. Going west from the summit the trail descends rapidly through jack pine thickets to a fairly large sized stream, at its present low stage 20 feet [6 m] wide and six inches [15 cm] deep, at high water its bed is probably 200 feet [60 m] wide in places. Three and a half hours travel down the bed of this stream brought me to the trapper cabin on the Sikanni. The river at this point is very swift and the valley very narrow and deep. Small 2nd growth flats probably several hundred feet wide occur at the bends of the river in places. Generally speaking, however, the sides of the valley extend to the river's edge from a height of approx. 1000 ft [300 m]. I followed down the river bank through the brush for about half a mile, where I camped and in the evening I observed Arcturus for latitude.

Travelling down the bed of the creek this PM I was unable to get any rabbits or chickens. I was fortunate however in clubbing 3 suckers at the mouth of the creek, 2 of which I had this evening and kept the other for the morning as I have nothing else.

At 4:25 AM on May 30 Milligan started for the cache on the Sikanni Chief River. Along the way, he surveyed another a loop connecting the North Pine and Sikanni Chief valleys.

Shortly after leaving camp I climbed the hill (1000 feet [300 m]) on the east side of the valley. A good view was obtained and useful bearings, notes taken in connection with the route survey…. From this hill I struck northeast two or three miles from the river to avoid ravines and then turned northerly parallel to the river and followed this course for the rest of the day…. Obtained a chicken and six eggs this morning, a rabbit in the afternoon, and a porcupine this evening so that the dog and myself fared fairly well.

Late that night he set up his tent about five kilometres above the cache. When he arrived at the cache on the last day of May he found everything as he and Cartwright had left it 10 days ago, but he noted: "The river … had dropped a little since we were here last. This would make travel downstream difficult so I decide to put in a day or so around here as these warm days should surely bring the snow off the hills."

While spending the first day of June in camp, Milligan had an exciting adventure.

Had a visit from a black bear this morning. He came within 20 feet [6 m] of camp before the dog and I noticed him. The dog barked and I got a flying shot at the bear as he scrambled out of sight in the timber and of course I missed. Many curses as the dog chased after him. By noon the dog hadn't returned so after following their tracks for about an hour I met him (the dog) coming back. I think the bear can run faster than Tomato, for which I am glad.

Milligan's next concern was for forest fires. On June 2 he wrote:

Sun is darkened by smoke from forest fires. The southerly and southwest wind is bringing cinders, etc. Burnt pine and spruce needles are noticed floating downstream.

This morning I made a trip about five miles [8 km] upstream and completed sketches of river valley. I also collected specimens of about a dozen different plants and grasses. Everything was gathered in indiscriminately. There are two or three different kinds of grasses, although no doubt very common variety I nevertheless couldn't name. It is my intention to collect if possible a specimen of every plant that grows in these parts and ship out for classification.

This afternoon I moved my camp downstream three miles [5 km] to Indian trail that leads out of valley westerly. I followed this trail this evening to the top of plateau 1200 to 1400 feet [350–420 m] above the river. The sides of the valley are clothed in green timber being mostly 4–8" [10–20 cm] spruce, poplar, [and] birch (mossy ground). On the top the country is broken and hilly, the greater part of which had been visited by fires and should the present encumbrance of windfalls, etc., be cleared off would make range – probably nothing else.

Dark clouds have been gathering all afternoon and when I got to the top of the hill a "life-sized" storm was in full swing. A gale was blowing from the northwest and dead trees were falling in every direction. I hope the result of it is rain so as to check the fires. The fires would travel for miles, as the country is very dry, having had warm days and no rain practically since the snow melted off in April.

The fires burnt as they are in muskeg and windfall I do not think would do much harm to the country. They would, however, seriously affect our travelling.

Fortunately, a heavy rain the next day dampened the fires and Milligan saw no smoke that evening. He spent the morning making rabbit snares and the afternoon setting them. Before moving on again, he needed food for Tomato, who had been getting "somewhat short rations for the last few days". On June 4,

> after collecting two rabbits from the snare line this morning I started downstream at 9:30 and at 9 this evening reached the Winter Quarters Camp. I was 8½ hours actual travelling, an approx. distance of 50 miles [80 km] by river which would give an average current for that part of the Sikanni of about five miles an hour.

The trip downstream was uneventful. With only one person, a dog and virtually no equipment, the canoe rode higher in the water.

The next day Milligan prepared for a trip "easterly through the country between latitude 57°45' and 58°". It rained almost all of June 6, so he remained in camp. "I took the Kodak to pieces this afternoon and after two or three hours' work on it managed to get it into working shape again, the trouble with it being that the works were clogged with the mud and silt from the river water." Now he would be able to make a photographic record of his explorations in 1914.

On June 7 Milligan left on his survey trip to explore the country east of the Sikanni Chief River.

> Two shots, two rabbits. Mosquitoes as ferocious as I have ever experienced them. After pulling the canoe up this morning I made up my packs with the following outfit and started on the trip to the headwaters of the Fontas River. Sextant, mercury, lynx fur robe, mosquito tent, two small pots, cup, spoon, knife and plate – which I also use to hold the mercury when observing – four or five pieces dried meat, tea, sugar, four cups rice, flour and cornmeal, barometer compass, etc., notebook, 30.30 rifle, and 20 shells and small axe – two pouchfuls Imperial mixture, also 18 rabbit snares.

He followed the trail they had used last fall for about 11 kilometres before turning to the east and travelling another 4 kilometres, where he camped on a "scrub spruce ridge".

During his travels the next day he found himself at Hill 2 and climbed to the top, where he could see much of the country to the north, west and east. This viewpoint assisted Milligan with his mapping, since he was able to see many features that he had previously surveyed, and it also provided him with a good view of the country where he intended to travel. He took bearings to the Fish Lake hills and other prominent hills, and sketched the Sikanni and Conroy valleys. Then he continued walking east to Conroy Creek. "The water was fairly low and I was able to wade, although too deep for the dog with his pack…. Immediately I left the edge of the bench on my easterly course I was once more in muskeg (scrub spruce) and continued so till 5 PM when I found a dry spot amongst a thicket by the side of a small creek that runs into Conroy." He used his rifle to catch more food: "three shells, three rabbits".

On June 9 Milligan estimated that he travelled east for 20 kilometres.

> I started out this morning in muskeg and camped in muskeg this evening, the only dry ground encountered being along a creek which I crossed about five miles [8 km] from this morning's camp. I passed (two miles up) by the north end of a ridge, evidently the last of the summit hills…. Along the creek mentioned the Sikannie Indians travelled evidently last winter as fresh chopping was noted.
>
> . Beyond a couple of old Indian trails running north and south and an occasional fresh moose track nothing was seen worthy of note - nothing but spruce and tamarac bog, two to three feet of moss.
>
> [I] observed the sun for latitude at noon and plotted my route survey this evening (so tired).

He hunted efficiently again that day: "three shells, two chickens, one rabbit."

The next day it rained for several hours so Milligan and Tomato walked only about 12 kilometres before their packs became soaked and heavy.

> About a mile from camp, after travelling through the usual muskegs (scrub timber) I came to a well-worn Indian trail going north and south. I followed this north for about a mile along a dense thicket maze sloping to the North, when I branched off to the east. After crossing a short muskeg I found myself in an entirely different sort of country – patches of poplar and jack pine with good clayish loam, this in places where the country has been burnt. Crossing over I travelled over jack pine ridges with muskeg between and still further east I came into scrub spruce and balsam timber with good stretches of alder bottom, soil excellent black loam. For the last two or three miles to camp I descended gradually from this timbered ridge thro scrub spruce and moss, a sort of semi dry muskeg.

June 11 proved to be a very good day.

> Snared two rabbits, three shells one chicken. A perfect day. As the sun rose this morning there was not a breath of wind nor a cloud in the sky, and the air seemed unusually fresh after yesterday's rain. As the day wore on cumulus clouds were noticed floating with a slight breeze from the north. These however disappeared towards evening and as I retire the sky is clear again with the exception of low banked clouds along the western horizon. The hum of the mosquitos outside my netting almost drowns the ripplings of Kahntah as it rolls by the camp.
>
> I reached the stream, which I take to be Kahntah River, at 4 this afternoon after having passed through a very pleasing country, in fact I consider it the most hopeful area that I have encountered since leaving the plateaux in the vicinity of Fort St John last year.
>
> After leaving camp this morning and making small cache of grub for return trip and taking two rabbits from the snares on the way I continued the gradual descent through 2nd growth willows, alder, pop, birch, spruce

thickets (occasional mossy patches) for a couple of miles to a small 10 feet [3 m] stream running northeast. Here I stopped for a couple of hours and observed the sun for latitude, my intention being to continue on today and tomorrow, blazing so that I could find my way back to the cache.

After hanging the sextant and mercury on a tree I proceeded. I climbed out of the creek ravine and was once more in timbered muskeg, truly it was disheartening. I seriously considered returning.

The swamp lasted only for about a quarter of a mile, however, when I began to ascend through spruce and balsam timber. Another ½ mile brought me to the top and down the other slope to the end of spruce timber. I was in the valley of Kahntah River, and for the three miles to the river I travelled through small poplars and willow with light windfall. In places I tried the soil with my axe and found generally two to six inches [5–15 cm] of dark loam (not exactly black) with clay subsoil. An occasional view was obtained from the open poplar slopes, and as far as I could see this entire valley is all poplar country. Looking back on the course I had come, it appeared that I had followed through the edge of the spruce timber, all the country to the south being poplar and willow.

So elated was I at striking this country that I forgot all about blazing so that I will have to be careful when I return. Along the banks of the stream are grassy flats ½ to one mile wide, covered in places with willow clumps and poplar, also standing dead stick and windfall, the soil excellent alluvial loam. The stream itself is about 50 feet [15 m] wide with dark brown water. There are slight rapids at intervals between which the current is sluggish. Set ½ dozen snares this evening.

In March, Milligan had been at the Kahntah River at its junction with the Fontas. This location was now upstream, further south.

He did not move camp the next day. "My ½ dozen snares caught only one rabbit and having only five cartridges left I did not risk moving ahead another day but set more snares this morning as I have got to have rabbits." He spent the afternoon cruising up the east side of the Kahntah River, noting:

The bench land above the river land is practically all good agricultural land, about 75% being poplar and alder and the balance moss covered with standing dead stick. The soil is all good.

Undoubtedly this poplar country was at one time scrub timbered muskeg. Here again fires have done good work. All this country has a gentle slope to the north and drainage of the remaining swamps would be a simple matter. On looking at my sketch map of the district I note that we passed through similar country 20 to 30 miles [30–50 km] south of here last year. It is probable therefore that this 2nd growth continues as far south as the summit. I regret [because of time and food constraints] that I

cannot go on farther into the next valley east as I would very much like
to determine the easterly limit of the good land.

On June 13, after collecting four rabbits from his snares, Milligan started
back to the Sikanni Chief River. He returned to where he had left a small
cache on June 11 and camped there, setting more snares in hope of getting
enough food for Tomato.

He followed his route back to the "old Indian trail" that he had crossed
on his trip east. This time he followed the trail as it headed south and west
for about 12 kilometres, where he camped for the night.

> This trail has been well cut out and has at one time been used as a horse
> trail. It has, however, not been travelled apparently for a number of years.
> Probably to avoid the wet mossy ground the trail keeps for the greater
> distance along the edge of a small stream along which are poplar and alder
> with excellent soil.... Under the moss there is good soil varying from light
> clayish soil in the pine to black humus loam in the scrub spruce. I am sur-
> prised to find such good country only two or three miles [3–5 km] south
> of the hopeless bog I had passed through going east.

> I may say that wherever the bog or wet ground occurs there is ice or
> frozen ground immediately under the moss, this I found when setting
> rabbit snares. I am of the opinion that when once the scrub timber and
> moss is cleared off and the soil exposed to the sun that this entire country
> would be equally as good as any of the excellent patches that are found
> wherever the ground is dry.

Milligan reached the Nelson trail early in the morning of June 16 and
"followed it 25 miles [40 km] to the Sikanni, arriving at 8 PM. I had hoped
to find horse tracks coming from St John, but in this I was disappointed.
Cartwright, however, should return any day now and I will take advantage
of the time till he arrives to get dog feed and work on the plans. I can't do
much on these, however, without an almanac. I can't do anything with the
sun observations."

Rain fell for the next two days, and Milligan wrote:

> I'm afraid that the rainy season has commenced in earnest, as it was just at
> this time it commenced last year.... [The] river has risen nearly two feet
> [half a metre] since yesterday morning. Set rabbit snares on the hill. Dur-
> ing the 18 days that I was away a marvellous growth had taken place in
> these parts. The grass along the side hills is in places a foot [30 cm] high,
> while on the timber flats the moss in places is almost hidden by a rank
> growth of gorse grass knee deep.

On the third day of rain the river rose another 20 centimetres. Milligan
tabulated his meteorological data, arranged plant specimens that he collected, and prepared some soil samples, all to go out with Hazen when he
arrived. He also collected seven rabbits from his snares.

June 20 brought rain for the fourth straight day.

> It struck me that some data as to the approx. amount of rainfall during this season might be of value. So this morning I constructed an improvised rain gauge and set it out on the beach at 10 AM. I obtained a piece of sheet iron from our old stove and shaped it into a funnel, rectangular shaped, with catchment area of 7½ x 10½ in or 78.75 sq. inches [508 mm²]. I placed this over a Worcester bottle previously measuring its circumference, also average thickness of glass (from another broken bottle) and thus obtained the inside section of the bottle to be 2.865 sq. in. [18.48 mm²], from which I gained that 1/10" [2.5 mm] of water in the bottle represented .00364" [0.0925 mm] rainfall.

The weather finally cleared the next day. Milligan was growing impatient for Cartwright to return, so on June 23 he started back along the Nelson trail to meet him. The next day he hiked another 30 kilometres without finding Cartwright. "[I] don't know quite what to do under the circumstances. I hate to think of travelling for a month in new territory without watch, film, almanac, etc. But I'll have to if Cartwright doesn't show up in a day or two." He continued on the next day, still with no luck. "Am forced to believe that something has happened and decide that there's nothing for me to do but return. The hard part of it is not the thought of travelling another month alone – it's being without film, watch, almanac, etc."

On June 26 Milligan gathered nine rabbits from his snares before leaving camp at 7 AM for the Sikanni Chief River. He left a note for Cartwright on the side of trail, telling him where he had gone. He planned to go downriver the next day to continue his surveying, but Cartwright arrived that night at 1 AM. He had found Milligan's note yesterday and hurried to catch him. He brought letters and some supplies. Fred Hazen arrived at camp the next evening with four horses carrying food and more supplies needed for the summer. He aslo brought with him Joseph Apsassin, a Dunne-za trapper who had worked for the Hudson's Bay Company at Fort St John and had a trapline in the area.

Milligan could now begin his summer explorations.

E.B. Hart

In the spring of 1914 Hart continued his exploration of the Prophet River area. While waiting for the ice to melt he built a spruce-bark canoe – he must have learned by watching First Nations canoe-makers. He launched the canoe on May 2 and headed for Fort Nelson. Two days later he arrived at the Hudson's Bay post. He spent a few days there, then "started down the Fort Nelson River, making a route survey of the same and checking up work done the previous year". He noted that there was no difficulty taking boats up or down the river: "I fancy that a properly built gasoline boat could run on this river at all times except that of extreme low water." He described the land along the river as "the same as those of the Prophet and Muskwa rivers, the bottom lands being covered with a heavy growth of spruce and cottonwood timber, the plateau being wet on either side".

When Hart reached the Liard River, he found it necessary to canoe down to Fort Simpson "to connect with the steamer from the outside, both for the purpose of getting mail and obtaining supplies for further work in the mountains, and also men to track the canoe up the Liard River". He reached Fort Simpson on June 18 and waited for the steamer. "For various reasons, the steamboat was delayed, being much later than usual coming down the Mackenzie, and I was delayed for three weeks at this point." During that time he hired Archie Gardiner to accompany him for the remainder of his exploration. The financial arrangement he made with Gardiner would later create controversy for the surveyor general.

Once the steamer arrived, Hart and Gardiner left by canoe, proceeding up the Liard River to begin summer explorations.

Summer 1914

G.B. Milligan

Milligan spent the first days of summer at his campsite on the Sikanni Chief River catching up on correspondence and planning his report to the surveyor general. On June 28, the day after Cartwright arrived, Milligan wrote a letter to George Dawson, summarizing his spring activities:

We left Fort Nelson last spring on April 9th and carried the survey south by Fish Lakes to the Sikanni River to connect up with the survey of last season. This was effected by an azimuth from a hill four miles [6.5 km] west of Fort Nelson to a point on the Fish Lake Hills, a distance of about 40 miles [64 km], latitude being obtained at each station. By a rough triangulation Fish Lake hills were tied to the end of last season's surveys on the Sikanni. As a result of this tie and shown on the rough sketch plan being forwarded under separate cover Fort Nelson is plotted approximately ten miles [15 km] east of its present position on the maps. Last season the survey was carried north from the Dominion Block to the Sikanni principally by route survey checked astronomically by observations for latitude and LMT from which differences of longitude were obtained. The longitude would thus be only approximately correct and an effort will be made to obtain a check when we work south along the easterly portion of the country.

On May 9th we started up the Sikanni by canoe, which we had built, making rough triangulation survey of the valley and its tributaries. About 40 miles [65 km] up, the river became very swift and we encountered a succession of rapids making upstream work very difficult and slow. The canoe was therefore abandoned and we struck across country to the North Pine to meet our man from Fort St John, whom I had written from Fort Nelson last January instructing him to bring mail including photo film, almanac, watch and several other articles that I required. We were disappointed in this, however, our man failing to show up. It was therefore decided that Mr Cartwright make the trip to Fort St John himself as it was imperative that I obtain the films and watch, etc. as the watch I had was put out of commission and what few films I had left were ruined in an unfortunate canoe accident on the Sikanni.

In the meantime I returned to the Sikanni and made an examination of the country to the west and also made a trip easterly across country about Latitude 57°50 to the Kahntah River.

Mr Cartwright had to wait at Fort St John till the 15th of this month [June], the mails having been delayed, my letter from Fort Nelson being 5½ months reaching Fort St John. Mr Cartwright returned here with packer and four horses on the 26th [actually June 27]. These return tomorrow and will take back specimens of grasses, etc., also samples of soils and coal.

Fine weather prevailed throughout April and May there being only five days in which rain fell and towards the end of May the whole country was very dry and bush fires were numerous. Growth made marvellous strides during May and June no doubt accounted for by the long days of warm sunshine and which in these latitudes compensates in no small way for the shortness of the season.

On July 2 Milligan finished his paperwork and Fred Hazen returned to Fort St John. Milligan was ready to explore the country to the north. In the

Milligan's dugout canoe on the bank of the Sikanni Chief River, along with a raft that he and Cartwright made to transport their supplies on the river. Some of their goods have been unloaded on the shore. RBCM PN3377a.

Sikanni River valley. BCA I-67823.

summer of 1913 he had surveyed mainly in the North Pine (Beatton) River drainage. He would spend almost all of the summer of 1914 exploring the Fort Nelson River drainage, which was larger and even more remote.

The next day he and Cartwright began canoeing down the Sikanni Chief River. They made several stops along the way, where Milligan "climbed the benches and sketched course of river, etc.". He noted "excellent growth of grasses on the side hills affording good range" and "timber on the river flats is mostly large cottonwood with 2nd growth spruce". They reached the mouth of Conroy Creek the following day. Milligan had hiked along the upper part of this creek while on the Nelson Trail.

On July 5, their third day on the river, Milligan made a "route survey of the river by compass and judged distance, the benches being too heavily timbered (with poplar and spruce) to permit long sights along the valley." He also sketched the spruce-covered flats. "Although the amount of timber increases as we go down, the valley is narrow and there is not the amount of timber that I expected. Where the river cuts into the sides of the valley cut banks are formed, generally clay with iron-stained crumbling shale."

The next morning they arrived at the mouth of the Fontas River, made camp, and spent the rest of the day surveying in the area. "I climbed the bench on the north side and with the small transit took bearings to the west and then fixed my position." Milligan was encouraged to see "excellent timber … at the junction of these rivers and up Fontas, good clear spruce average two feet [60 cm] in diameter and running up to 100 feet [30 m]." He continued to take observations on the sun and the stars for his surveying. But his reduced equipment for this summer forced him to use the sextant for taking sun shots, which made his work more difficult. "Observed sun for latitude and time, but there being a slight breeze, the mercury was not steady, so I waited till night and observed the stars." Milligan and Cartwright remained at camp the next day "and counted 130 trees to the acre [320 trees/ha] averaging at least two feet [60 cm] in diameter by 80 to 100 feet [24–30 m] high."

The two men met some First Nations people that day. "As we were preparing to leave for upriver this morning 10 canoes (spruce bark) loaded with Siwashes came down. They were all practically starving having been unable to get any moose. We traded tea, etc., for moccasins and gloves. We obtained useful information about the country – trails. They told us the water would be too low for our canoe." The group camped next to the surveyors that night.

On July 8 Milligan and Cartwright began travelling up the Fontas River.

The water is dark brown and a remarkable contrast is noticed where the waters of the two rivers meet – the Sikanni loaded with silt and Fontas clear brown water. Before we left this morning the Indians caught two large fish coarse variety (apparently jack fish) about 2½ feet [75 cm] long using large hook and sucker as bait. The current of the river is very sluggish, not more than ½ mile an hour and we were able to pole or paddle upstream without difficulty. At its mouth the water is about 10 feet deep [3 m] and gradually becomes shallower as we go upstream till about 10 miles [16 km] up we had to abandon canoe travel on account of not enough water. In ordinary seasons, however, there would be quite enough water according to the Indians, to canoe up as far as Kahntah River.

In the afternoon Milligan climbed a bench on the north side of the river that was about 100 metres above the river. From there he was able to get a good view up and down the river and sketch the topography.

The next day: "After caching what we couldn't pack we started upstream with four days grub intending to make the junction of Kahntah where I had left a cache last winter. Kept a route survey and estimated we travelled about 12 miles [20 km]." Milligan noted: "Without doubt the timber on this river is the finest I have ever seen in the north", and estimated the trees to be 50 to 100 centimetres in diameter and up to 30 metres tall.

The two men hiked another 20 kilometres the next day.

About 11:30 we struck an old Indian trail which led up river and which helped a lot. Good timber prevailed throughout the flats.... In places recent fires had burnt the poplar side hills and penetrated in spots to the timbered flats. In my opinion fire protection throughout this corner of the province is badly needed as it would be a pity should the timber be lost as it will prove a valuable asset to this country in view of scarcity of timber east of the Rockies.

The Fontas River. LTSA.

On the fourth day they reached the confluence of the Fontas and Kahntah rivers. This was the farthest Milligan had travelled from Fort Nelson
during the winter. He had made a track survey from Fort Nelson to this
location and taken an observation for LMT (local meridian time) when
he was here in March. In the spring he had run a triangulation network
between Fort Nelson and the camp on the Sikanni Chief River. And on
this trip he had made a track survey from the Sikanni Chief to this place,
thus completing a large triangle in his surveying network that encompassed
three important locations. Once again he took an observation for LMT.

Beyond the confluence of the Fontas and Kahntah rivers Milligan was
surveying new country and hoping to reach the Hay River.

> On the north bank of Fontas I struck an old trail which led me up-
> stream and across to the Ekkaantah River [Ekwan Creek] near its junction
> with Fontas which little stream I continued up for several miles when I
> climbed the open poplar bench on the north side of the valley. Splen-
> did views were obtained up and down stream (photos taken). The valley
> bears N80°E and as far as I could see the country has been fire swept, the
> growth being now small poplars and willows with scattered patches of
> spruce. Fontas valley above Ekkaantah is about ½ to ¾ mile [~1 km] wide
> between benches which rise 100 to 150 feet [30–45 m] above the river.
> The river itself is not more than 60 feet [18 m] wide with dark brown
> water. Ekkaantah about 40 feet [12 m] wide (same kind water) flows from
> the north or northeast and joins Fontas about a mile above Kaantah.
>
> Unsuccessful attempt to obtain time shot on stars owing to passing
> clouds.

Milligan described July 12 as "a perfect day" and he measured the sun's position for LMT before leaving camp in the morning. "The greatest part of this country has been recently burnt over and it is most difficult to follow the old trails through the downed timber and brush." The first trail the men followed led instead up the Ekwan Creek valley. The next trail went up the Fontas valley.

> Owing to this country having been fire swept the trail was difficult to
> follow, and after going up Fontas valley a couple of miles I lost confidence
> as I had understood from the Indians that the trail turned abruptly away
> from Fontas. It was decided to camp and this afternoon we cruised the
> bench to the north of Fontas and after a little scouting discovered what
> we suppose is the Hay River trail.

Here he noticed that the Fontas was becoming shallower and swifter.

Their difficulties in travelling continued the next day.

> Four miles [6 km] along the Hay River trail this morning brought us to
> fork, one trail going north. and the other southeast. We followed the one
> going north for about 5 miles [8 km] when we got into a tangle of wind-
> fall and we thought it wise to return especially as I thought that going due
> north wouldn't take us to Hay River.
>
> We arrived back at the forks again at 5 PM and took the southeasterly
> trail. After following this for 2½ miles [4 km] it petered out altogether and
> we camp this evening in the "middle of nowhere".

Later, in September, Milligan would find that the trail to the north led to the Hay River, though it appeared to be heading in the wrong direction.

> One consolation in chasing up these old trails we have discovered a
> very fine stretch of country. The intention is to continue southeast for the
> next couple of days and then return this way again and I hope to obtain
> some idea of the extent of this country.
>
> With the exception of occasional patches of swamp the country
> travelled today is all good poplar and willow with a large percentage of
> meadow. Along the meadow is found a luxuriant growth of wild hay in
> places 5 ft [1.5 m] high. The soil in the meadows is several inches of black
> loam with clay subsoil while amongst the poplars it is chiefly clayish or
> sandy loam – all supporting a good growth of grasses, etc.

Trail conditions did not improve on July 14.

> Shortly after leaving camp this morning we got on the old trail again
> and followed it for about ½ mile southeasterly through the poplars and
> willows when the country changes entirely and we find ourselves in an
> almost impassable bog (spruce and tamarac). We followed the trail (appar-
> ently used only in the winter) for about 3 miles [5 km] farther when the
> bog got from bad to worse so that we were continually sinking up to our
> knees in the muck. Bulrushes, slough grass, etc., grow to height of 4 feet

[1.2 m] amongst tamarac. We were forced to stop at a point where the blazes led across a large almost open marsh bog, over which travel is impossible at this time of year. We returned by the way we came and cruised the poplar country to the northeast and estimated the extent of first class land to be between 20,000 and 25,000 acres [8,000–10,000 ha].

On July 15 Milligan decided to continue up the valley of the Fontas, noting that "the river is very crooked and winds in about every direction of the compass". The upper part of the Fontas flows from the southeast, running almost parallel to the Hay River but about 10 kilometres west. There was no distinct height of land separating these two valleys and the men could not find a trail.

The following day the men explored different areas:

> From camp today Cartwright cruised for several miles on either side of the river while I put in the day up river. North of the river on the plateau Cartwright found spruce and tamarac bogs while on the south the country was better, being poplar spruce and birch with light soil. I continued the route survey up the river. Several miles up the river forks, the main or larger stream turning east (or northeast and southeast). I continued along the plateau between the two streams for a couple of miles and then turned east to the east fork where I observed for latitude at noon after which I continued northeasterly and returning at 4 observed for LMT. From the point where I took the observation I struck across country northwest to west and came out ¼ mile [400 m] above camp at 7 PM.
>
> Up as far as the forks the river flats (or points) are covered with alder and willow all good soil.… On the north side of the valley spruce and tamarac bog extends for miles and in places is about impossible to travel across. Time and again I would mire down almost above the knees.

Milligan had explored a new area of his survey, one that had proved difficult for travelling. Although he was not far from the Hay River drainage, one of his major objectives for 1914, he had not been able to reach this area because of the trail conditions and his uncertainty about which of several trails to follow.

On July 17 he and Cartwright started back to their cache, but did not get far. "After … about 2 miles I pulled out my watch to note the time in connection with my route survey and found that it had stopped. It took me till 4 o'clock to get it going again after taking out several hairs that were tangled up with the works. We travelled till 7:30 in the evening and estimated the distance six miles [10 km] for the day." Since Milligan's watch was important for recording the time in his sun and star shots it was imperative to fix it as soon as possible. Once it was working again, Milligan reset his watch according to the time on Cartwright's (he had given his second watch to Hart) and the last recorded time difference between the two. For the next few days he wrote a daily comparison of time between his and Cartwright's watches.

The next day they reached the confluence of the Fontas and Kahntah rivers.

> The intention was to follow the river back but it became so crooked that we had to abandon it and strike north to the trail. The country has been burnt along the river and for short distances back from the top of the bench back to the muskegs. Looking north these muskegs or swamps appear to be limitless, probably extending as far as the Ek-kaantah River [Ekwan Creek]. The fact of the Indian trail to Hay River going east for four or five miles [6–8 km] then due north would justify this.

On July 19 Milligan and Cartwright explored more of this fire-swept country, both for mapping and in an effort to find the best routes for travel.

> Cruised for trails up Kaantah and Ek-kaantah rivers for trip tomorrow. In the morning a good trail was found going southeasterly from the mouth of Kaantah. I followed this for few miles across fire-swept plateau through poplar and willows. This would be excellent country if it were not for the rocky soil. I had more difficulty in PM endeavouring to find trail up Ek-Kaantah. The country being recently burnt is now almost impassable owing to windfall and dense brush and I was unable to pick up any Indian trails so tomorrow I will have to follow up along the bench on the north side of the valley.

The next day the two men again explored separately.

> Cartwright examines country to the southeast while I put in the day up the Ek-kaantah. Leaving the timbered river flats and mounting the 200 ft [60 m] bench to the plateau the country is found to have been practically all burnt over and with the exception of isolated patches here and there the original growth of timber has disappeared and small poplars alders and willows now grow in place.

Milligan provided a generally bleak description of the Ekwan Creek area.

> The valley of Ek-kaantah varies from 1 to 2 miles [1–3 km] wide – Benches diminish from 250 ft [75 m] at the junction with Fontas to 50 ft [15 m] 15 miles [24 km] up. The first few miles have been fire-swept recently – the tangle of fallen spruce and large poplar with rank growth of grass and weeds makes travelling difficult. Farther up the valley, swamps are frequent, being mostly scrub spruce and tamarac. Along the sides of the valley and for some distance back from the bench, the ground is dry and good poplar and spruce country is found, soil sandy or clayish. The Ek-kaantah River is very sluggish and in places appears more like a stagnant slough than a river. It has a width of 20 to 30 feet [6–9 m] and a depth of 2 to 6 ft [60–180 cm]. The stream in places is almost choked with reeds and moss, etc. Evidence was found of canoes having been used many years

ago on this river. This fact, also that old beaver dams were found where now the ground is high and dry, would justify the belief that the country is drying gradually for to be able to use canoes on the river it would have to be cleared of reeds, etc.

On July 21 Milligan made an observation for LMT before they began their return trip to the mouth of the Fontas River. They travelled about 23 kilometres on the trail and "camped at point where old trail comes to the river from the north. This is the trail I had followed from Matsula's camp to the banks of the river last winter."

The two men had to stay at this camp for a second night. "Watch stopped last night making it necessary for a trip back to the cache for another time observation." Fortunately for Milligan, his watch had stopped near one of his main survey locations in the area. Since he had previously made observations for latitude and longitude at this station he could re-establish his position and reset his watch. "I started back with sextant 7 AM, arrived at the cache at 12:20, observed at 3, and returned to camp at 9 PM. In the meantime W.H.C. cruised plateau – both north and south of the valley and takes three photos."

About 24 kilometres of travelling the next day brought Milligan and Cartwright to the place on the Fontas where they had left the canoe and cached supplies on July 9. Milligan noted the change in vegetation that had occurred during the past two weeks. "Slough grass, etc., were 5 ft [1.5 m] high and difficult to wade through. Rank growth of grass and weeds is found all along the river flats."

On July 24 the two men arrived at the point where the Fontas and Sikanni Chief rivers meet to form the Fort Nelson River. Milligan had made a route survey as they travelled down the Fontas and now made an observation of the sun at the confluence.

The next day Milligan and Cartwright started down the Fort Nelson River in their canoe and continued on July 26 until strong wind and heavy rain forced them to set up camp in the afternoon. The rain continued next morning, so Milligan set out the rain gauge he had made and recorded 1/10 inch (2.5 mm) per hour. That afternoon they resumed travelling downstream, camping near the mouth of Fish Creek. From the bench on the south side of river Milligan had a good view and noted: "at the bends of the river where the stream cuts into the timbered flats large trees have fallen into the river and these, anchored by the roots in the channel, present obstacles to navigation." He also made a latitude observation at noon to verify his route survey.

Midday on July 29 Milligan and Cartwright stopped at the place where the winter trail left the river. They had been here in December while on their way to Fort Nelson and again in April on their way back to the Sikanni Chief River. In the afternoon, they continued on in their canoe and reached Fort Nelson in the evening, where they found "all of the Indians of the district encamped here awaiting the arrival of the H.B. scow and treaty party and who were now two days overdue. As a result the Siwashes are on starvation rations, no tea, tobacco, and [they] are reduced to using flint and steel for matches." Although the First Nations in the Fort Nelson area had only joined Treaty 8 a few years previously, the arrival of the scow with supplies and the annual payment of treaty money had already become an important occasion.

Milligan had returned to Fort Nelson to get more supplies for the remainder of his exploration, to send a letter to the surveyor general and to collect mail. More importantly, he wanted to find someone to guide him to the Hay River, since he had been unsuccessful in reaching the area by himself. The gathering of First Peoples gave Milligan an opportunity to find a good guide. He spent the next day developing his photographs and found that his camera was working again after its dunking in the Sikanni River a few months ago. Since he had sent out his photos before leaving Fort Nelson in April, he had only lost the pictures that he took in early spring and had only been unable to use his camera for about a month. (Later, when he returned to Victoria, Milligan took his 1914 photographs home. He and Cartwright used some of these pictures in their reports, but most did not go to the surveyor general's office and have been lost or destroyed.)

While waiting for supplies to arrive, Milligan decided to do a route survey down the Fort Nelson River to the Snake River. He took a First Nations guide with him and they reached the Snake on August 1.

> On the way downstream this morning we stopped at the Slavie [Dene-thah] camp for an hour till the rain lessened. Great were the entreaties for tea and settoo [sugar] and though I only had a very little myself I couldn't refuse old Fontas [also known as Fantasque] who had taken me out to his camp on Sahtaneh (Bear trail) River last winter. We arrived at Snake River about 3 PM and made camp about ½ mile below its mouth. I obtained an observation for L.M.T. and spent the rest of the afternoon on back observation. Below the Muskwa the Fort Nelson River increased in width to about 300 to 350 yards with a current of about 2 to 4 miles [3–6 km] per hour. A rank growth of grass and weeds and berries of all kinds are found along the river flats which entered in places from ½ to ¾ mile [~1 km] to the foot of the bench. Excellent timber is also found on most of the flats. This is being noted in course drawn with the route survey.
>
> Two Indians camped at mouth of Snake River have fish nets out in eddy of the Nelson. They catch principally suckers, big jackfish [northern pike] and other coarse varieties. Obtained an approximate latitude from altitude of Polaris (el-lah-cho hooley).

August 2 was a "a fine, sunny day" and Milligan spent it studying the land to the northeast. He noticed how fire had benefitted the growth of plants, and his view of the region was much more optimistic than it had been the previous summer.

> In places openings occur generally [as] results of fire, and here is found a most luxuriant growth of grasses, weeds and berries bushes, etc. This growth is from 4 to 6 feet [1–2 m] high and the Indian paths around places where they have camped appear as tunnels or lanes through the rank growth.

> Proceeding from the river flat following an Indian trail northeasterly I climbed the bench (made 250 ft [70 m] high by barometer) to the main plateau. From the edge of the bench I travelled through alders with good black loam for a couple of miles and then into more open poplar and willow country which had been burnt over not many years ago.

> For the remainder of the day I travelled through the same burnt poplar all with rank growth of grass and fireweed. The soil is all clayish loam and in many instances where depressions occur in the gently undulating surface of the plateau, the water from recent rains lies on the surface except of course where the mossy swamps occur the water apparently being taken up by the moss. About five miles [8 km] and I came to the edge of valley Sahtaneh River. The west slopes were open with scattered poplar. From openings that I passed through during the day views were obtained of the surrounding country and as far as I could see this plateau region where it had been fire-swept was now all good poplar and willow country. Occasional mossy swamps occur, but this season being fairly dry these swamps seem not nearly so formidable as they would otherwise.

> The whole country at this season of the year presents a most pleasing appearance and one cannot but imagine a great future. We have had no frost this summer and the rank growth seen everywhere would justify the belief that at least practically everything that is grown in other parts of our northern interior could be grown here.

The following day Milligan and his guide began the return trip to Fort Nelson, arriving at mid afternoon on August 4. "On the way up we stopped off at the Slavie [Dene-thah] camp. Here there were about a dozen different camps and probably 30 Indians. I counted no less than 18 canoes on the banks all in readiness to go upstream when the transport arrives."

On the evening of August 7 Ed Heron, the post manager, "arrives with his family in Peterboro canoe and informs me that two barges of supplies will be up in the morning, the delay being caused by the Mackenzie River boat being over a week behind time. Heron brought up tea and tobacco – and this evening the natives are happy once more."

As promised, the Hudson's Bay Company boat arrived the next day with the treaty party.

George Milligan, front and centre, with First Nations men at Fort Nelson. Photographer unknown; BCA A-04248.

We were awakened this morning by rifle shots outside, in front of the building. Following an old custom they were greeting the crew on the barges of whom there were 26 all told, the majority of whom were taken from here last June. Answering shots from the crew could be heard at intervals around the point about 2 miles from the Post. They finally arrived at about 9 and with much solemn hand shaking all around greeted the crowd on top of the bank. Mr Camsell the H.B. inspector and his family also came up.

[The next afternoon] a "big feed" was held … in which all the Treaty Indians participated, tea, flour, beans being supplied by the Indian Department. The only Indians of the district who aren't paid Treaty money are Matsula and his two wives.

[The following day] the Indians hold a "tea dance" in the evening and continue till 8 o'clock next morning.

Milligan wrote a letter to the surveyor general to send with him downriver with Arthur Camsell.

Although I will regret very much leaving the country without having been over it all, I nevertheless hope that by the time we start for the Coast this fall sufficient information will have been gathered, so that the report as finally sent in will give some idea of the general character of the country in this corner of the province and its possibilities.

The country travelled this summer has been a great improvement on last season. In fact there are large tracts of good country that would compare favourably with anything I've seen in the North. It is not by any means a prairie country, but the soil and growth in places especially along the river valleys is excellent.

In winding up this season I plan to go from here next month to the Hay River and then work south to its headwaters where I expect to meet Cartwright who would come north from Fort St John with horses. We would then return to Fort St John, probably by beginning of November. I would thus be in Victoria early in December.

It was now almost mid August and Milligan had only about two months left for his explorations. While there were so many First Nations people at Fort Nelson, he tried to obtain their assistance. He had not surveyed much territory northeast of Fort Nelson and particularly wanted to visit Kotcho, the largest lake in the area; he had also not reached the Hay River area. But his first priority, while there were still some Sekani at the fort, was to find someone to go south with Cartwright to their fall 1913 camp on the Sikanni Chief River. His initial arrangement failed when "the Sekani chief's son ... was declared by his father to be too sick to travel, so another Indian, Ho Ho, was persuaded to go along with him." Milligan was fortunate to make this arrangement, because shortly afterward, "Bellyful pulled out with his women folk for Fish Lake and several other Sekani followed".

Milligan talked to Matsula, who had been one of his guides during the winter. At first Matsula agreed to help him with a trip to the Hay River, but the negotiations soon became more difficult:

Matsula was approached today [August 13], at what was thought an opportune moment, in regard to packing out a party for me to his camp on Hay River, the parcel containing supplies, etc., for my trip from his camp to the head of Hay River. Matsula was much opposed to the proposition, as his dog, being in poor shape, and also his outfit had quite all they could pack of their own stuff. In an interview with Mr Heron he expressed himself rather loath to help the white men.

Mr Heron told me afterwards his reasons being that Hart had set him against us last spring. When he [Hart] had hired some of his band to pack stuff to Fish Lake and after all arrangements had been made, moccasins built, etc., Hart backed out without paying them for the trouble they had already gone to. This is a small thing in itself, but with an Indian like Matsula, who needs careful handling, it makes it so much harder for the next man who requires his help.

Milligan was successful, though, in finalizing his arrangements for Cartwright's trip to Fort St John: "Two Indians will travel with him as far as our old winter quarters camp on the Sikanni. Upon his arrival at St John he will secure Joseph Apsassin as guide and with several horses travel north to the headwaters of Hay River where I expect to meet him from this end."

On August 14 "most of the Indians who have done their trading have pulled out for their hunting grounds" and "Cartwright finally got away today with his two Indians at about 4 o'clock." There was also an important development for Milligan. "Matsula made peace today and sent his boy for my pack. He also said he would do what he could for me in the way of showing me around his country." Milligan began preparations for the trip. The next day he "observed for LMT in the morning and afternoon." Since his surveying station at Fort Nelson was the prime one for his survey he wanted to make as many observations there as possible, especially because he was about to survey a new area. "Matsula got away this afternoon with his band and said that if I left tomorrow I could easily catch him up as with the women and kids they don't go very far in a day."

Milligan began his trip east on August 16.

> Settled accounts with Heron this morning and finally got away about 11. Mr Heron was good enough to send his man Tom with me to Matsula's camp on Snake River where we arrived this evening at about 5 PM. Here we found about 7 different camps, the elite of the Slavie tribe [Dene-thah], and I was very glad Tom was along with me, as I felt somewhat embarrassed amongst so many people whom I could not talk to.

For the first part of the trip Milligan followed the same route as he had on his visit to this area during the winter.

> A most agreeable impression, as to the plateau country, was left in my mind as a result of the 11 miles [18 km] easting we made today. On leaving the post and reaching the plateau, I found, although I'd been over the ground last winter and more or less condemned it, that the grass was excellent and the ground underfoot was drier than I had expected in view of recent rains....
>
> The predominating soil throughout is ... clayish and is no doubt accountable for the water from recent rains lying on the surface almost everywhere.... About half a mile distant on either side of the [Snake] valley the flats are open and covered with a most luxuriant growth of grass 2 to 5 feet [60–150 cm] high. I am told that several Klondikers put up hay at this point and wintered large number of horses.

The Dene-thah held their camp for another day while the men went hunting for moose, but they returned in the evening with only rabbits and a porcupine. While they were out Milligan explored the land east of camp. "[I] found that these open hay lands extended for ½ mile east and the same north and south, apparently being muskeg that had been burnt over by frequent fires, and even in places the grass is now growing through the old half burnt off moss."

On August 18:

> Moved camp today about six miles [10 km] easterly across the unlimited

Fontas (also known as Fantasque or Fontah), a leader of a band of Dene-thah in the Fort Nelson area, when he first met Milligan in the previous winter. LTSA.

plateau. Travelling as I am with these natives would afford plenty of opportunities for a real live journalist. I regret my incapacities in this line. The camp was astir about 5 AM and soon after their breakfast all the male members of the crowd were off ahead with their guns and rifles and a light pack. The women were left to follow with the camp outfit. Old blind Fontas was led by a small boy who led him by a string. His task in getting over the trail was not an easy one. 75% of the country travelled today was wet, mostly mossy. In places there were bogs where grew bull rushes and long grass.

The greater portion of the country has been burnt over, some places the country is open and grassy, in others covered with dead stick and also there were patches of green spruce, alders etc. All of it was wet however and a good deal boggy.

On August 19:

We crossed only one swamp today and that extended for the 5 miles [8 km] that we made from this morning's camp. We didn't go far but travelling over the swamps was not easy and I was glad when a halt was called when we came on to firm ground on the banks of Ootaan Dezie★.... In a very wet season like the summer of 1913 I can well imagine that it would be a difficult country to get over. As it is the water lies ankle deep practically everywhere.

Matsula had success hunting that day and he gave Milligan a special treat.

Matsula came in this evening with the biggest part of a moose on his back. He was out only the half day and said that he had tracked the moose a long way across windfall country and finally came onto it as it was about to bed down. The moose nose and tongue he fed me with great ceremony, and although very nice I wouldn't consider the nose the great delicacy that they do.

The group had only a short journey the next day, but everyone was busy.

Another short move of three miles [5 km] brought us to the junction of trails to Kotcho, where camp was made. The men went out for the rest of the day on a hunt but returned this evening without seeing any moose tracks. All the women went to point where Matsula killed moose

---

★ A *dezie* is a waterway like a creek or river.

yesterday and packed in balance of the meat. I made a cruise a few miles north of camp.

The trail followed today through mostly firm ground amongst spruce and poplar, along the banks of Ootaan Dezie. The old and romantic trail of '98 was taken part way and the old pack saddles etc. gave evidence of the Klondikers having passed this way.

Leaving the camp and going north from the creek I found myself once more in swamp. Nearly all of it is scrub spruce and mostly burnt. Where there is grass there is water on the surface and where moss the water has sunk, or taken up by the moss.

Heavy rain the next day forced them to stay at the same camp.

The natives waited till the late afternoon when they suddenly realized they were out of meat and so all the men started out with their packs and I was allowed to go with them. No sooner had we started than it commenced heavy rain which kept up all evening. Everything miserably wet. For the few miles travelled we were on dry ground along banks of Ootaan Dezie. Burnt poplar country, good sandy clay soil.

The rain continued on August 22.

Nothing was done till 3 o'clock when being out of meat we had to shift along, although it was raining, a misty drizzling rain, the kind that penetrates. New trail had to be cut most of the way through fallen timber and bridges built across the swollen creeks. We therefore made poor time and camped about 5:30 at the crossing of Ootaan Creek. As soon as we arrived, the Indians went out hunting, returning at dusk with rabbits, chicken and squirrels enough for the evening meal.

Milligan described the area through which they travelled. "The trail was never far from the banks of the creek and avoided swamps. Fires had burnt off the original growth and poplars and willows have sprung up along the creek presenting a hopeful appearance. The wet country however is not far away, generally ¼ to ½ mile."

The weather cleared, so the men went hunting early the next morning.

Matsula, failing to return this evening, is reported to be on the trail of a moose. The balance of the battalion, the women and dogs moved up to the camp today. I suggested going on a bear hunt with a couple of the Indians but was told "tu thlon dooyea" [too much water; it will not be easy★], so took the hint and went on a cruise of my own north of camp. I found the usual thing – dry poplar country along the creek and swamp behind.

Though August 24 was a "fine clear day", the group covered only 12 kilometres over swampy terrain.

★ Translation by Dene-thah Chief James Ahnassay.

Water on the surface everywhere except on narrow poplar and spruce ridges we crossed in passing from one muskeg to another. The country appears to have better drainage facilities as numerous small streams flowing southerly have considerable fall. I spent the afternoon cruising to the south and for most of the time managed to keep clear of muskeg. The country has been burnt and dead stick and windfall amongst poplars and willows spruce is usually found.

That evening Milligan attended a special ceremony.

When I returned to camp I found moose and therefore starvation was postponed for a time…. A great feast was held in the evening at old Fontas' camp at which I was presumably a guest of honour as I was given a place beside the chief and was fed the "delicacies", viz the nose, tongue, etc. After the feed Fontas gave us some very impressive music on the drum, which was apparently appreciated by his large audience (of 22 males). The women, by the way, did not participate in the feast. It was apparently only given to the hunters of the band. During the course of the evening a vote of thanks was tendered the "moola" for having helped out the Indians with tea tobacco, etc., at starvation time before the arrival of the transport [in Fort Nelson]. Although I have seen quite a lot of the Indians of the north, their drum music, dances and gambling, etc., this evening's ceremony is one that will live in my memory for some time.

The next day the Dene-thah remained at this camp.

The day was spent drying moose meat and scraping the hides. All the men except Matsula went out hunting and in the evening returned with only rabbits and porcupine. I observed for latitude and LMT and spent the balance of the time with Matsula who seemed unusually willing to give what information he could viz the extent of muskeg country, course of streams, the trail of the Klondikers and names of streams, etc. It is principally by signs that he tells me all this; of course he talks all the time and with the few words I know I manage to understand a good deal of what he tries to tell me.

The group resumed travelling the next day.

Moved another eight miles [13 km] across the plateau. The practically dead level plateau of the last few days changed today to slightly undulating country. Although fairly well drained by numerous small creeks there was nevertheless considerable swamp. The water from recent rains lies on the surface giving the appearance of swamp where there would be excellent country in dry season.

Practically all the country has been burnt and small poplars willows are growing up amongst standing dead trees and windfall…. Along the creeks is good growth of grass and pea vine and pine grass, fireweed etc. amongst the timber.

Tenday Nadilla returned this evening with portions of a large bull moose he had killed.

There is evidently a sick person in the camp as old Fontas spent the evening "making medicine", a weird and noisome performance. I did not interrupt him as I understand strangers are not supposed to witness an affair of this kind.

The next day they walked only about five kilometres to a creek, and from there blazed a trail to the place where the moose was killed. "The undulating country of yesterday changed to rolling today, therefore the better drainage. The muskegs have disappeared except small patches here and there. The country has all been burnt at one time and willows and poplars grow amongst standing dead spruce, poplar and windfall." Milligan used the time to explore the country north of the camp, where he found similar terrain.

The group remained at this site a second day.

I spent most of the day trying to arrange for one of the band to take me over the country. I'm quite satisfied that the Indians are now quite willing to help me in any way they can but when it comes to discussing an extended trip across country everything is "dooyea" (very hard), "ditchen thlon, tu thlon, dooyea". Money seems no great object with them – to hunt and stack up the moose meat for the winter seems their only concern. I finally, however, managed to arrange with Matois to take me over a branch trail northeast to a stream called Clee Cho Dezie (Horse Creek).

On August 29 Milligan and Matois walked about 30 kilometres, reaching Horse Creek by mid afternoon. Milligan noted that the terrain "was practically free of muskeg" and "with the exception of the top of the ridge … was excellent country. The detour we made to the east and then north was necessary to avoid a particularly dense stretch of windfall."

It rained the next day, so they remained in camp. Milligan explored the area nearby, noting that it lacked prominent hills from which to obtain a good view of the country. The virtually flat terrain meant that all of his surveying in the area east of Fort Nelson would have to be by route surveys, which were not nearly as accurate as triangulation surveys. The lack of views prevented Milligan from making sketches of the geographical features of the area and limited the type of photographs he could take.

On the last day of August Milligan and Matois returned to the Denethah camp and found that they had moved on to Kyklo Creek about 50 kilometres away. "From the trail forks to Kyklo the trail makes many deviations from the general direction to avoid the masses of fallen timber. We came to the camp on Kyklo Ck without having made any perceptible descent. The stream appears to flow along the surface of the plateau, the valley being wide with only slight slope gives this impression."

Milligan began September by securing guides for two trips.

I made arrangements today whereby Matois leaves with me in the morning for a fortnight trip east along Kyklo R. to Kotcho River, then up the latter to Kotcho Lake and thence to Fort Nelson to meet the Treaty Party on September 15th. I was also successful in negotiating with the wily Matsula to take me up the Hay River in the late fall. All this required a little diplomacy and considerable patience and I retire this evening well satisfied with the day's work.

[The next day,] with our packs of dried meat, fat and tea, [Matois and I] left the Indian camp at 7 this morning, and taking the trail down Kyklo River we made about 17 miles [27 km], camping at 5 PM. Ky-cho Deah (or Little Hay River) is about 30 ft [10 m] wide and at its present stage is about 4 to 10 ft [1–3 m] deep it being in flood owing to recent rains. It flows at rate of about 1½ mile [2.5 km] per hour and winds its way entirely through what appears to be a wide shallow valley.

Milligan believed that the land along the Kyklo River would be good agricultural country.

Grassy meadows, willow clumps and poplars, 2nd growth spruce poplar and also a large percentage of burnt over country where is now dead stick windfall, willow etc. The soil is good, clayish.... On either side of the river extending back for 10 to 15 miles [16–24 km] the country is almost flat with only a small rise. Muskegs are found, also considerable wet windfall country. The Indians out hunting moose in these parts are often in water up to their chests half the time.

The night was clear, so Milligan measured the position of Altair for latitude.

On the morning of September 3 he and Matois crossed the Kotcho River. Downstream this river joins the Hay River just inside Alberta. Instead, the two men headed upstream, toward Kotcho Lake.

Kotcho River at this point is about 50 feet [15 m] wide with a current of 2 to 3 miles [3–5 km] an hour and depth of 2 to 6 feet [60–180 cm]. Along its banks are some fairly good sized (2 to 3 ft) spruce trees that had somehow or other managed to escape the fires that swept over this entire region. One of these trees we felled across the stream as a bridge....

[Then we] followed a small stream for 4 or 5 miles [about 7 km] along which were excellent grassy meadows and willow and poplar country. The grass is 2 to 4 ft [60–120 cm] high and would make excellent hay. We came to the banks of Kotcho River again about 1 o'clock (observed for latitude at noon) and following it up for about an hour we stopped and made tea. From this point the trail swings to the East of north away from the river. A couple of hours through windfall and swamp, through belts of spruce and the muskeg, through alders [and] willow where there was

practically no trail, brought us to a small stream flowing southeast and here
we made camp. The swing to the northeast, my guide told me, was made
to avoid almost impassable windfall country near Kotcho River.

After hiking about five kilometres the next morning Milligan and Matois
reached "the 'Clee-cho-etannie' horse trail which was found to be going
N30°W". Milligan was again on the trail that the Klondikers had travelled
16 years previously.

Taking the horse trail (the old trail of '98) we travelled for an hour
N30°W through excellent country, willows and poplars with large extent
of open grass land, soil black loam and clayish. We stopped for tea at 9 and
put up the fly as shelter from the driving rain. We delayed here several
hours till the storm lessened when we continued on again. About a mile
and a half [2.5 km], all through good willow and poplar country, brought
us to the point where the horse trail of the Hay Lake Indians swings to
the north and east and crossing Sheekeelia River and heads for Hay Lake.
This horse trail finds firm ground by following around the top of a rise or
swell in the plateau. My guide, who knows this whole country, informed
me that the old trail of '98 crosses Kotcho near Townsoitoi Dezie and
follows for most of the way along Sah-cho Creek (Grizzly Bear Creek)
where the country is fairly dry and growth [of] poplars and willows.
Indications proved that the Hay Lake Indians had been over this trail
recently with horses.

North and east of Sah-cho Ck the country rises gradually to summit
between the waters of the Hay and Bescho Rivers. For miles and miles
the country has been fire swept, and is now difficult to travel, owing to
windfall (tdar thu). It would almost appear that what is now required is
more fire to clean off the fallen timber.

Leaving the Hay Lake Indians' horse trail we turned more to the west
and for the rest of the day followed the Klondikers' trail. Over swamps,
through dead stick country, through patches of willow and poplar and
windfall, across bogs where still were the old corduroy, some in good
condition, we continued till 5 PM when we came to a small stream where
we made camp. This point was designated "Recuperation Camp" by one
party of Klondikers who had left a message dated July 23/98 on a blazed
tree to the effect that everything was OK except that they had lost a horse
in one of the swamps.

On September 5, about an hour after starting, they reached the Kotcho
River again.

Here Matois was doubtful as to where the trail continued and so went
a cruising while I did "le tea cluatze". Along Kotcho River at this point
is an excellent growth of grass for probably a couple of hundred feet on
either side of the stream while beyond which the country varied from

dry willow ground with dead stumps and burnt logs to mossy dead stick muskeg.

Matois located the trail and they continued north.

At about 10:30 Matois sighted fresh moose tracks and after examining these [and] the willows where the moose had been feeding, he said that the moose had passed by yesterday and that it wouldn't be very far ("netha ille"). He took off his pack and with his rifle went off on the moose tracks. Before he returned, which he did about 1 PM, and without the moose, I had had time to observe the lower limit of the sun for latitude.

Then the two men continued walking north until about 4 PM, when they made camp.

Matois went off on a hunt. The country travelled this afternoon was fairly good, for the most part being poplar and spruce thickets with the usual percentage of swamp.... 80% of the country has been fire swept and the dead fallen timber over which we had to scramble made travelling slow. Matois returns this evening without any meat. He set 11 snares for rabbits on the trail ahead.

The next day they met some animals, but not the species they had been hoping for.

Got tangled up with a pack of wolves this morning, which afforded some excitement. We hadn't been on the trail more than half an hour from camp when fresh wolf tracks were seen. The grass, etc., along the trail was beaten down by the pack that had passed along and Matois exclaimed "dee ghi thlon" (many wolves).

When we came to the banks of Kotcho, Matois examined the tracks and said the wolves were "netha illez" (very close). He concluded that they had just killed a moose judging by the hair etc. on the trail. Shortly afterwards Matois sighted the wolves, ahead amongst burnt timber about 50 yards from us and he immediately commenced blazing away at them with his .44. Out of the nine shots he fired he killed two and badly wounded three. He could have got more but had none too many cartridges to take us to Fort Nelson.

In the meantime I had been viewing the scene from behind and when Matois fired the first shot the woods seemed alive with wolves and I judged there must have been 30 or 40. They were mostly black with several greys. They all started off at about the third shot but many came back again when the wounded ones howled. After a few more shots, however, they decided to move along. They didn't seem in any great hurry, but kept along the trail for about an hour when we noted they had got on the fresh tracks of a moose and followed it to [the] northeast.

We travelled through an indifferent sort of country today. Along Kotcho River the ground is firm amongst spruce and poplar, but the trail, when it swung away from the river, generally found muskeg swamps. 75% of the country is wet or mossy. In places along the river were thickets of 2nd growth spruce and poplar where the trail was quite distinct. A lot of the country has recently been burnt over and the trail was difficult to follow. Even Matois, who knew the country by heart, would often lose the trail and we would have to stop while he cruised around amongst fallen timber or swamps.

After passing through about 2 miles [3 km] of wet muskeg we came to Kotcho River at the point where the trail crosses it. Here we found the bark canoes with which the Indians had told me I could cruise Kotcho L. I was disappointed in this as we found the canoes full of holes and all warped out of shape. We did however find the cache of dried suckers that Matsula presented to me and these were most acceptable, and not only for the dog. We made camp in the middle of a muskeg about ¼ mile south of the lake.

As the largest lake in the region east of Fort Nelson, Kotcho Lake was an important location for Milligan's survey, so he established latitude at night using Altair. Then he and Matois spent a day exploring as much of the lake as they could on foot.

I was surprised to find Kotcho Lake so large. It lies about N°30W and must be 15 to 20 miles [20–30 km] long. My guide told me it would take 10 days to walk around it, this owing to the swampy nature of the country surrounding it and also time would be lost bridging the streams that flow into it. I took bearings to the prominent points, etc. and sketched the lake roughly noting two islands, one good sized, about four miles to the north, and the other the same distance N12°E. I regret very much at not being able to put in more time around the lake, but being almost out of meat we have to move on and in this vicinity there is very little game. Flocks of geese were seen, but these were always flying high and heading south.

Matois was able, however, to give me considerable information as to the nature of the country and he informed me that with the exception of a line of low hills which could be seen lying north and east to the east of the lake, that the entire country was muskeg. Very little more can be said except that most of the country, muskeg or otherwise, has been burnt over and the hills mentioned are difficult to travel owing to windfall.

On September 8 Milligan and Matois started back to Fort Nelson, following the Klondike trail.

We travelled till 2 when we came to a likely spot for rabbits and made camp. I observed the sun for LMT. Country travelled today was very swampy and I marvel how the Klondikers ever got over it with their horses and cattle. A good deal of the country has been burnt and patches of poplar country with windfall are found between muskegs.

The next day there were

no rabbits in the snares this morning, so we tightened our belts and "hit the trail". About 20 miles [32 km] across the wet plateau and we were ready to stop. The snares are again set out along the trail ahead. Along Sahtaneh Ck, which we followed for considerable distance, the trail was fairly dry through poplars, willows and spruce. The wet windfall or muskeg country is never far from the creek.

On September 10 they had better luck. "Caught one [rabbit] in the snares and shot two. We made good time today and got as far as Ootaan Dezie, several miles beyond the junction with Matsula's trail. Today we had the usual wet burnt windfall country, patches of muskeg between ridges of spruce and pine."

On their fourth day from Kotcho Lake Milligan and Matois reached Fort Nelson.

My trip back to Ft Nelson was made principally in order that I could, through an interpreter, arrange with the Indians to take me up the Hay River this fall, also that I might send out films by Treaty Party when they return to Simpson. I've told the Indians that I am going to make the trip whether they help me or not. They seem willing enough to do what they can, but living from hand to mouth as they are and also there being a scarcity of young men in the tribe who know the country I want to travel, each eligible hunter has a family to feed and it is difficult for them to get away for any length of time and again the rabbits dying off makes it more difficult.

Arranged to have new dog pack made. Obtained Indian names of streams and English equivalent. Observed sun for LMT.

On September 13:

a few of the Sekani Indians arrived today for "Treaty" and brought note from Cartwright stating that he reached the horse trail OK. In discussion with several of the Indians regarding the invasion of the Klondikers through this country in '98 I learn that the season they came through was an exceptionally dry one and in spite of this a large number of horses were lost in the swamps.

The next day, the Indian Agent who was due did not show up, and neither did the Dene-thah from Matsula's camp with a package of film that Milligan wanted to send out by mail. When the agent still had not arrived on September 15 Milligan decided leave the next day for Matsula's camp. He would try to arrange for a guide for the Hay River trip without an interpreter. There was insufficient time to explore more of the country northeast of Fort Nelson, so this was Milligan's last objective. He wanted to be able to determine how much of the Hay River was in British Columbia, chart the course of the river and see if, as rumoured, there were any lakes in the BC section of the waterway. This area had not been reliably mapped, so Milligan wanted to do some surveying there before heading south to Fort St John.

He and Matois left the post on September 16. "Matois says he [Matsula] should be camped at the junction of Kotcho and Kyklo rivers. We travelled 25 miles [40 km] and camped at our old camp near Ootaan Dezie." The next day they walked another 30 kilometres. "The last few days the leaves (foliage) have noticeably changed from green to yellows, red, gold and orange. Matois notes this with misgiving as he says when the leaves are all gone the bull moose are no longer fat and meat without fat is worse than bread without butter."

On their third day from Fort Nelson, after hiking another 40 kilometres, the men reached Matsula's camp but not where they expected to find it.

> When we arrived at Kyklo Dezie we found a cache of dried meat …
> and fresh blazes leading up Kyklo River on the south side. A slip of paper
> with Siwash (hieroglyphics) thereon explained to Matois that the Indians
> had passed by five days ago, the reason for their retreat from the country
> to the east being that they were unable to get any moose and being hun-
> gry they returned to where they knew there were moose.
>
> Matsula explained to me this evening that, although there were a few
> moose tracks, the wolves were so numerous they were forced to give up
> hope of getting moose in that vicinity.
>
> I am very pleased, however, to see that their camp poles are loaded
> with meat, they having just recently killed 5 moose. It affects my plans not
> a little as without meat in the camp I would have little hope of getting a
> guide for the Hay River.

Now that he had arrived at the Dene-thah camp Milligan had to see if he could find someone willing to guide him into the Hay River area. The next morning

> Matsula informed me … that there was no dried meat in the camp and
> that it would be best to wait for a day or so as the meat would be that
> much lighter. They will also require time to make moccasins and fix dog
> pack, etc. I discussed the subject of guide but the Indians are not at all
> keen. I still have hopes, however, that they will arrange that one of them
> will come with me as far as Kaantah Dezie.

Negotiations continued the next day.

> The Indians had evidently discussed the guide matter amongst themselves
> and through Matsula informed me this morning that it was impossible to
> provide a guide as it meant the loss of one of the moose hunters and there
> being only one to each family and also that they had to hunt every day to
> get the moose while they were still fat it was out of the question for one
> to leave for any length of time. They said it was not a question of money

but that they had to think of their families first. A lot of Siwash rot and I would have told them so if I'd known enough of the language.

I told Matsula that I was going to make the trip in any case and that if I couldn't get a guide I would leave in the morning and ferret out the trails myself. The matter stood at this till this evening when I was called over to a "big feed" at the chief's camp where [there] were the five head of the band. They endeavoured to persuade me to abandon the Hay River trip, as alone, I would have difficulty in that windfall country as the old trail would certainly be obliterated, etc., etc....

I told them I was leaving in the morning whereupon after more discussion about the police etc. if I were lost, Matois finally spoke up and offered himself at $5.00 a day. It sounded a lot at first but I realized after a little thought that it was worth it, as I know, that without a guide it would take me some considerable time to get through to Kaantah Dezie. After much ceremony the matter was finally closed. Matois said he would require tomorrow to get moccasins made, etc., and that he would leave the day after – the 22nd.

The next day Milligan found that his arrangements still weren't finished. All the hunters of the band went off on a two or three day moose hunt today and before going Matsula offered me his small 12-year-old boy to accompany Matois at $5.00 a day. They seem to think I've more money than sense. I finally closed at $30 for the trip, which will probably take 10 days. I've also bought a dog at $15.00.

On a sunny September 22 Milligan finally began his trip to Hay River. Matois and Daelie, (Matsula's boy) and myself left the Indian camp this morning at 7 with our packs loaded with dried meat and grease and tea. 5.8 miles [9 km] a little south of east along Kyklo R. brought us to junction with the trail from Ft Nelson. We made about 16 miles [26 km] today following the same trail along the South side of Kyklo R. that Matois and I took on our trip to Kotcho Lake. The reason for naming the stream Kyklo [grass or hay] is apparent in the rank growth of hay along the banks.

The next day they continued east along the trail for about 22 kilometres to the crossing of Kotcho River, the place where Milligan and Matois had turned north to Kotcho Lake on their last trip. Now Milligan would be travelling through territory he had not yet surveyed.

I observed here for LMT at 2:30, after which we continued on. Crossing the stream we followed an old trail along the North side for about 3½ miles [5.5 km] and made camp. For the entire distance we travelled through good country. With the exception of patches along the stream where there were few spruces, the country has all been burnt over, and where frequent fires have burnt off the fallen timber there is excellent growth of grass 4 to 5 ft high. The soil is mostly clayish.

He described his explorations of the area in detail.

Seven miles [11km] easterly along good trail brought us to the junction with the horse trail going southeast to the Hay River and northwest across the Kotcho River to Kotcho Lake. This is the trail taken by the Klondikers in '98.

We delayed at this point an hour so that I could observe the sun at noon for latitude. The entire seven miles was through good country along Kotcho River.... We crossed trails where beavers had been at work on Kotcho.... Occasional muskegs were crossed but not of any great extent. I followed the horse trail North for a short distance to the Kotcho River at this point entirely blocked with windfall....

Leaving Kotcho River we took the horse trail southeasterly and about 3 miles [5 km] brought us to Townsoitoi River, a stream 20 ft [6 m] wide and 2 to 4 feet [60–120 cm] deep. This stream drains wet country west and north of Ekwanten [Ekwan Lake], and flows into Kotcho R.

Here we branched off the main trail and followed upstream a few miles to an Indian camp where the Indians were hunting beaver. We camped here for the night and had moccasins mended, dog pack repaired. These Indians had not a morsel to eat in the camp, not even tea. But they hoped to get a beaver this evening or in the morning.

From Kotcho to Townsoitoi Rivers the country rises gradually through mostly wet swampy country. A couple of photos I took will give an idea of the muskegs, some of which are nearly open, others covered with dead stick. As a general rule, however, the wettest ground is found where there is dead timber and grass, this would be good land if drained.

They reached the Hay River on September 25.

Leaving the Indian camp this morning accompanied by the 3 hunters of the band we returned downstream to the horse trail and followed it south of east for several miles to a slough near the Hay River where tea was made and I observed for L.M.T. The trail followed entirely through poplar and willow along Townsoitoi for about a mile then swung more south, crossed a muskeg through a clump of spruce and then across a large hay meadow probably 640 acres [260 ha] in extent. Many hundreds of tons of hay could be cut on this flat. I took a photo of it. After tea we moved on several miles more across more hay meadows and poplar and willow country to the main trail that follows up and down the Hay River. Here we hung up the greater part of our packs and taking only enough grub for a couple of days we left the other Indians and turned down the Hay River. I hoped to get as far east as the boundary and then return and go up the Hay River. This trail has not been travelled for a year or two and was partly blocked with fallen timber & together with the growth of red willows, rose bushes and cranberries, travelling was slow and we had gone

The Hay River valley. BCA I-67825.

only about 5 miles [8 km] when it was time to camp. Along the river are large spruce and cottonwood, also large poplar. A lot of good timber has been destroyed by fires and the remaining timber, although of good size (2 to 3 ft [60–90 cm] diameter) did not appear to be of any great extent....

Continuing downstream this morning [September 26] the trail crossed about 1½ miles [2.5 km] from camp to the south side and a little further on we stopped, and leaving our packs, I cruised ahead for 3 miles and returned and observed the sun for latitude at noon.

At his furthest location downstream Milligan was about five kilometres from the Alberta border. Since the boundary between the provinces had not been surveyed in this area he would not know its exact location.

At this point fires have cleared a large extent of country where now is excellent land, willows and poplar with excellent soil. Along a small stream paralleling the Hay River large quantities of excellent hay could be cut. A couple of photos were taken which should give some idea of nature of country.

In the afternoon we returned upstream, picked up our packs, and travelling several miles till we came again to the Hay River, we made camp. I observed Altair this evening for latitude....

The most significant feature of this river is that it has no defined valley. The stream itself is about 100 feet [30 m] wide and at the present stage there is not enough water to float a light canoe over the bars. It flows in a most winding course and is sluggish. Its current is not more than 1½ to 2 miles [3 km] an hour. It would no doubt be a different story at high water in the spring or after a spell of rainy weather, and at this stage, the Indians'

Matois, Milligan's guide, in a meadow in the Hay River valley. LTSA.

yarn about having floated 5 days downstream without being able to land owing to flooded banks may not be an exaggeration.

Milligan wrote about the Hay River and its valley.

On either side ... the country is practically level as far as one can tell. It is very well named the Hay River as not far from its banks for the whole distance I have travelled are numerous meadows varying in size from 100 to 500 or 600 acres [40–240 ha]. They are usually crescent shaped and lie parallel to the course of the river. This fact would lead one to believe that at one time the river flowed where these openings occur. The growth of hay on these meadows I have not seen equalled anywhere. In places it is 5 to 6 feet high and so dense as to be difficult to travel through. It is like breaking trail through 2 feet of snow. Surrounding these meadows and along the banks of the river is a growth of large spruce cottonwood and poplars. Recent fires have destroyed a lot of this timber and evidently made travelling difficult owing to windfall.

Referring again to the meadows, many of them surround small ponds or sloughs and others are dry. This is a good duck country in the fall and large numbers were noted, especially on these sloughs.

The next day Milligan and his guides continued about 23 kilometres up the Hay River through similar terrain. "The country rises gradually as we go south and the Hay River with the small creeks flowing into it have benches on either side about 30 ft [9 m] high. We found today the usual proportion of hay meadows, sloughs, burnt tracts around which detours

Ekwan Lake. LTSA.

were made to avoid the mat of fallen timber, and also spruce country with moss covered ground."

On September 28 Matois took Milligan on a side trip to the largest lake (except for Kotcho) in this area.

> Travelled 18 miles [29 km] today and camped at the south end of Lake Ekwanten [Ekwan Lake]. For the first 5 miles [8 km] we continued along the Klondikers' trail up the Hay River valley to another trail going northeast across the Hay River to the Hay River post and west to Fontas River. The good country continued this far but when we turned west and climbed the 150 ft [45 m] bench from the Hay River we found ourselves once more in scrub spruce and tamarac swamps....
>
> From Kotaleen Creek till we came to Ekwanten we travelled through indifferent country, mostly spruce and tamarac patches of which had been recently fire swept and the resultant windfall was piled many feet high in such a tangled mass that it was found advisable to make detour around sand channel picking up the trail again on the far side.
>
> Within a mile of the lake we came onto good poplar and willow country where the original spruce etc. had been cleared off by repeated fires. The trail came to the lake about ¼ mile up from the lower end and when we broke from the timber to the open grass surrounding the water we sighted a moose at the south end. We opened fire at about 300 yds. but caused no damage. The moose however made matters easy for us and came around the end of the lake towards us. The dogs this evening had all they could eat and so did we.

The group remained at Ekwan Lake for a second day. They made a cache of the moose meat that they could not eat nor carry with them. Milligan observed the sun at noon for latitude, then took photographs and described the lake.

> Ekwanten Lake lies about N25°E and is about seven miles long and ¾ to a mile wide. It is called Ekwanten as it is supposed to resemble the shape of a shoulder bone of a moose – I failed, however, to see the connection. About 3 miles [5 km] up from the south end it forks into 2 arms, one going N20°E and the other about N60°E. Duck are plentiful on the lake. The lake is fringed with a growth of tall grass or reeds, tall enough to almost completely conceal a moose. North and west from the lake the country is very wet and bogs and grass swamps are frequent.

The last day of September was clear and warm.

> Moved on today 14 miles [23 km] to Fontas River. I shot a bull moose at this point and we made camp. In the evening I went out to our old cache at Kahntah River and taking tobacco and a little flour I returned to camp. Nine miles from the lake we came to the forks of the trails where Cartwright and I had passed last July. I hung up most of my pack here as this is my starting point for the trip across country to St John.

With the help of his guides Milligan had made one more loop on his route survey. This one, from Fort Nelson, connected with the survey that he had made into the area from the Sikanni Chief in July. In the process he had been able to include two new and important geographical features: the Hay River and Ekwan Lake. Milligan and Cartwright had been close to both the Hay River and Ekwan Lake during the early summer, but had been unable to navigate through the tangle of trails in this fire-swept country.

Milligan described the land. "From Ekwanten south the country is level. Large tracts have recently been burnt and we travelled for probably an hour in one instance through burnt country where the old trail had been completely obliterated. This is the point where Cartwright and I had turned back not having a guide."

October began with a clear day.

> I paid off my guides today and returned with the two dogs to my pack at the fork of the trails. They made a cache of the moose meat this morning and continued northwest by another of their trails back to their camp on Kyklo Ck. Matois, who is really a splendid type of Indian, gave me what information he could of the country I would pass through. His knowledge was limited, however, as he had travelled it only once, on a beaver hunt, and that was a long time ago.

Milligan had achieved his objective of reaching the Hay River and was ready to finish his exploration by heading south to Fort St John. He hoped to meet Cartwright and Apsassin along the way in the Hay River area.

E.B. Hart

After leaving Fort Simpson in June, Hart did not send any further reports to the surveyor general. In his final report he wrote a few pages about the last six months of his expedition. He described the Liard River on his return upstream, beginning at the 60th latitude, where he hammered in a stake on the bank of the river. He thought that the river valley had potential both for forestry and for agriculture.

> On this stretch of the river, from the boundary to the Fort Nelson River, there should be 100,000 acres [40,000 ha] of good spruce timber, running from fifteen to twenty thousand feet to the acre [11,000–15,000 m/ha]. In addition to this, there are probably twenty-five or thirty thousand acres [10,000–12,000 ha] of dry bottoms covered with willows and alders, which could be easily cleared and made fit for cultivation. The banks average from fifteen to twenty feet [4.5–5.0 m] in height above the river, and are composed entirely of alluvial soil, only one rock exposure being observed, and judging from the appearance of small Indian gardens on the river thirty miles [50 km] above Fort Liard, no difficulty should be experienced in growing all ordinary crops.

Hart also believed the river would be a good waterway for transportation.

> There is a good depth of water in the river practically everywhere from the Fort Nelson River to the Mackenzie, and there is no reason why good-sized power boats should not run on this river at any stage of the water. With the exception of one place thirty miles above Fort Simpson, where there are fifteen miles of rapids, there are no rapids on the river, and even in these rapids there is a good channel and no difficulty is experienced in taking up loaded scows.

When he reached the Toad River, he found it too swift for canoeing, so he headed cross country along the west side of the valley, picking up the river again about 30 kilometres upstream.

> The whole country, up to the head of the canyon of the Toad River, which it runs through in cutting the foothill range, has evidently in the past been covered with a growth of large timber, but this has been burnt off by the Indians, and as the Indians are dying off and are no longer in sufficient numbers to cover this country – no Indians having been in this particular section for at least forty years – I found it entirely covered with an impenetrable tangle of willows and alders through which I was compelled to cut every foot of my way, it being impossible even to force my own way through or to get dogs through with packs on, and in a month's hard work I only succeeded in making forty-five miles [70 km].

Just north of Beaver Creek, Hart discovered

> an extraordinary spring of perfectly black water. At first I thought it might

Toad River. E.B. Hart photograph; LTSA file 6952S.

be a spring issuing from a carbonaceous shale bed, but on examination I
found that it was running over a light, coloured clay and left no deposit or
sediment whatever. I had no bottle or utensil in which to collect any of
this water, much to my great regret. I tasted the water and found it to be
very palatable; in fact it was a favourite place for the moose to gather.

He commented on the potential of a dam for electrical power at the
canyon of the Toad River:

> If, in the future, developments in the north should warrant the expendi-
> ture, a dam could be constructed in this canyon two hundred feet [60 m]
> in height, which would impound the water of the Toad River, the Racing
> River and its eastern tributary for more than twenty miles [30 km] on
> each river, and afford electric power which would be distributed over a
> tremendous area.

But he noted one drawback: "If such a dam were ever to be constructed
in the future, there would be destroyed some 300,000 acres [120,000 ha] of
good farming land on the Toad and Racing River."

Hart visited and marked on his map an important site on the Toad River
that he had missed on his trip through the area in 1913. On the west side
of the Toad, at the mouth of the Racing River, he found a large hot sulphur
spring. He did not provide any further details in his report, but later he described the hot springs that he visited on the Toad and Liard Rivers to an
unnamed writer who published a brief article in the January 1926 edition
of *Popular Mechanics*, the well-known American science magazine.

Legends of a "tropical valley" in the extreme northern part of British Columbia where orchids and wild honeysuckles grow in rich profusion near mountains capped with ice, have been verified by official reports from Maj. E.B. Hart who was commissioned to make a survey of the province. His findings, now on file in the archives at Victoria, not only substantiate the tales of Indians and trappers who described the valley and its 300,000 acres [120,000 ha] of good land, but explain the apparent mysteries of its mild temperature. Hot spring, extending along the course of the rivers, Liard and Toad, literally steam-heat the valley so that even in winter the depth of snow is not over six inches while less favoured areas are blanketed to a depth of three or four feet. In season, upon bottom lands, are found luxuriant pine grasses, pea vine and lupines with an occasional orchid, while scattered growths of poplars attain a diameter of fifteen inches. Maj. Hart attributes the springs to weak spots in the earth's crust.

Hart's information provided more awareness of the hot springs in this area of northern BC. In 1931, Dominion land surveyor Knox McCusker guided the Mary Henry family from Philadelphia, Pennsylvania, who came to this area on a botany expedition. They were also searching for a "tropical valley" that they had heard about while visiting Jasper, probably the Liard Hot Springs. The BC government provided the Henry family with a copy of Hart's map. With the assistance of the McDonald family, local Kaska people, McCusker and the Henry family found the Toad River hot springs and made a film of visiting this site.

Because Hart had travelled through the area upstream from the hot springs during the summer of 1913, he moved as quickly as possible through this section of the Toad River. He continued his exploration in the river's headwaters, first following a branch that entered from the west. Here he reported: "[the] mountains are capped with lime, and there are evidences of mineral. In a wash of the creek entering from the east, near this point, I found copper float, and up the river on the west fork I found galena and silver chloride." Hart's discovery of copper was noted in a BC Department of Mines report in 1944, and there has been mineral exploration for copper in that area.

Then Hart crossed a divide to a lake at the head of the west branch of the Rabbit River. "Returning to the Toad River I followed it [the main branch] to its head, which I found to be interlocking in latitude 58°17'20" with the west fork of the Kechika. There, he completed his exploration in the fall of 1914.

Fall 1914

G.B. Milligan

At his campsite on the Fontas River, George Milligan prepared to return home. Along the way to Fort St John he planned to conduct a route survey that would make a large loop back along the eastern section of his exploration area to one of the survey posts on the boundary of the Peace River Block. He would make observations on the stars and sun whenever possible so that he could determine his position as accurately as possible. Latitude was particularly important on this trip, for it would help him determine the divide between the watersheds of the Fort Nelson and Peace rivers, and it would tell when he was back in surveyed land. He intended to meet William Cartwright and Apsassin, the guide, on his route along the Hay River.

But before he could begin, Milligan had to find a pocket compass that he had lost. He hiked back to Ekwan Lake and found it where he had chased one of the dogs to prevent him from getting a face full of porcupine quills. The detour of about 30 kilometres there and back meant that he started south at about 3 PM. "Made about three miles [5 km] and camped at spot where Cartwright and I camped last July [15]." For the first part of the trip Milligan followed the route he and Cartwright had taken in the summer when they attempted to reach the Hay River area by themselves.

He described what he had to carry to sustain him for the next few weeks.

Both dogs are heavily packed and I have all I want myself. My outfit consists as follows: silk fly, lynx paw robe, sextant, thermometer, pocket compass, barometer, watch, almanac, map, notebook, observation book, Kodak & about 10 rolls film, some exposed, package of original field notes, mercury, certain papers, seven pair moccasins, two pair sox, matches, tobacco, axe, rifle, 50 rounds ammunition, small frying pan, cup, saucer, hunting knife, sewing kit, 2 lbs sugar, dried meat, grease, a little fresh meat, five lbs flour, two pots, flint and steel.

He travelled about 20 kilometres the next day, October 3, and camped again beside the Fontas River.

> I followed an old Indian winter trail bearing roughly southeasterly. At about 8 o'clock this morning I came to the point where Cartwright and I had turned back owing to impassable bogs. I found these somewhat drier this trip, and by following the hummocks between the bogs where I could, I managed to get through the worst of the swamp by 9 AM. This is one of the worst bogs I have experienced and in spite of the recent dry frosty weather on many occasions I would sink up to the knees in the water and muck.

In the afternoon conditions improved.

> I continued in alternate swamp and spruce and tamarac and dead stick muskeg till 1 PM when the trail led up a slight rise, all fire swept. Here the soil appears to be good clayish loam. The entire country, muskeg and all, has been fire swept and the resulting dead scrub spruce standing at all angles, some already blown down, give an appearance of great desolation. I took a photograph of a typical bit of the fire swept moss country. The moss in places is quite 3 to 4 feet deep. About 2 miles [3 km] before I came to Fontas River I entered spruce and pine country. There were also some good stretches of willow and alder bottom with black loam between the ridges of pine.

His campsite on the Fontas was only a few kilometres upstream from the farthest point east that he and Cartwright had reached on July 16. "Obs[ervation] on Altair this evening made me in Lat 58°17'14"approx."

October 4 was "another clear fall day", but Milligan did not cover as much distance as he had planned. "Made about 10 miles [16 km] today, would have made more as I ran into a moose about 3 o'clock and spent the rest of the day hunting the dogs. I was also delayed tracing the trail; the Indians leave few marks on a winter trail." Initially the trail followed along a sandy poplar ridge near the river, but when it veered away he had difficulty finding it. He noted that the trail crossed "1½ miles [2.5 km] of very wet country. Beyond this was alternate muskegs and poplar and willow country. The country rises steadily as I go south." This was a hopeful sign that he would start entering drier ground that would make his route easier.

The next day he lost the trail completely.

> The Indian winter trail this morning degenerated to a blaze now and again and being too difficult to follow I took a direction of my own about southeast. As might be expected I got into difficulty before I had gone very far viz windfall and dense thickets. I came to a fork of Fontas River going south of west where I struck it, when I thought all the streams in

these parts ran north. I camp on this fork this evening and observe Altair
for Lat.

He was still in the Fontas River valley and needed to travel farther east to
reach the Hay River, where he planned to meet Cartwright and Apsassin.

He was encouraged to find the land rising in altitude as he progressed
southward, getting drier and easier to walk on; "although there are large
patches of muskegs (moss 2 to 4 ft deep, dry now) the country generally
improves".

Though October 6 was "a perfect day – cloudless and sunny", Milligan's
experiences were somewhat less than perfect.

I haven't much to say in favour of the country travelled today. With the
exception of a strip of willow meadows along a small creek (shown on
route survey) and also a patch here and there where fires have cleared
off the timber and grass has taken roots, the whole of remainder is scrub
spruce and tamarac muskeg.

I struck an old Indian trail in above mentioned creek but it took me
to the west and I had to retrace my route and only lost time thereby. I am
still on Fontas River waters where I camp this evening. This stream will
probably eventually head partly in Alberta [a correct assumption].

He met another moose the next day.

Continued today on a course of south, a little East. I reached Fontas River
a little after noon and continuing across I ran into a huge bull moose –
just what I wanted, as I had got down to a few pieces of dried meat. The
moose was not more than 60 feet [18 m] when I fired and the brute went
down like a log. To make a long story short, the moose, after a struggle or
two, got up and plunged out of sight into the timber and left me wondering what had happened. I only wish I could get over windfall country like
a moose. I must have hit him too high or too far forward in the shoulder.

I lost the rest of the day tracking the moose and waiting for the dogs to
return which they did about camping time.

While camping that evening, he climbed a tree to get a better view of the
land. "I recognized to my southeast a hill which I described in my report
of Oct. 13 as a low hump that rose above the surrounding country. It was
estimated in the vicinity of the Alberta boundary." Milligan had seen this
area over a year ago when he was looking northeast from the summit of
the divide between the North Pine and Sikanni Chief rivers. Now he knew
where he would be going.

He described the area he travelled through over the next two days:

75% of the country has been burnt and the resulting windfall is most difficult to travel through, especially for the dogs. Fontas River at this point is
about 60 feet wide and flows in a ravine about 120 feet deep and ½ mile
wide. Along the river bottom are fairly large spruce trees, while along the

edge of the benches on either side is a fringe of pines, behind which is the brule [burnt wood].

Continuing south this morning I crossed about 4 miles [6.5 km] of burnt spruce and tamarac swamp to a ridge timbered with large spruce and poplar. I got into burnt swamp again on the south of the ridge and came to another line of low hills lying about east and west. Here I struck an old horse trail going west of south. This trail has not been travelled for years, abandoned probably owing to windfall. I lost considerable time trying to trace the trail through the brule and finally left and struck south over the ridge and ran into the trail again at camping time.

The country has now changed from the level plateau to rolling country traversed by ridges running in almost any direction. On the ridges is a heavy growth of spruces (2 to 3 ft). Practically all of this has been killed by fire and the windfall is piled many feet high. Small patches of green trees are encountered and here the timber is good clean 2 to 3 ft spruce. Between these ridges the country is invariably swamp and also mostly fire swept. Probably this part of the "Empire" would be suitable for nothing but range after the dead timber has been cleared off. Moose are plentiful.

Milligan's campsite on the evening of October 8 was almost on the Alberta border. He had left the Fontas River valley and was heading south. Milligan realized that he had not made it over to the Hay River which only came into British Columbia for a short distance, and that he had probably missed his rendezvous with Cartwright and Apsassin. But he also knew that as long as he continued south he would probably reach the hill that he had seen a day earlier, and eventually arrive at the Peace River Block. Fortunately there had been no rain to slow his progress.

The next day was "practically a repetition of yesterday's except the ridges are closer together and the swamps between narrower. I lost time trying to trace the old trail and finally gave it up entirely and struck south over the ridges." According to the expedition map Milligan was travelling just inside Alberta for most of the day.

On October 10:

The country changes to 2nd growth jack pine with dense thickets of alder (mountain). It was here that I struck a good horse trail going southwest for first few miles then swinging to the south. It was a good trail and I was able to make 50% better time, the dogs not being bothered with windfall…. The general contour of the country is broken by ridges. Observed Altair for latitude this evening and patched my clothing.

As he walked farther south Milligan found the trails to be more distinct and easier to travel on. He also began to recognize features from his explorations during the previous summer.

Leaving camp and after passing through ½ mile of scrub spruce moss country the trail passes up on to a high jack pine ridge (jack pine and alders). My view to the east was blocked by another timbered ridge running northwest and southeast. To the west I could distinguish that part of the summit we had travelled in summer of 1913…. Continuing south I passed over several more pine ridges and on the top of one I came to forks of the trail. I took the trail going southeast and which had evidently been travelled by the Indians last summer.

By October 12 Milligan had been on his route for 10 days and knew that he had covered a considerable part of the distance south.

Yesterday I estimated that the summit hills were about 10 miles [16 km] south. I travelled 18 miles [29 km] today (14 miles [22 km] due south) and there is no sign of the hills. I travelled almost due south along good horse trail over fairly good country, practically level, to a 50 ft [15 m] stream flowing easterly. By fairly good country I mean there was only small proportion of swamp. Although 50% is moss covered spruce, poplar and pine the soil is good clayish loam. After crossing this stream the trail forks, one going southeast and recently travelled by Indians and the other going west. I took the latter as I wanted to get back to BC. It went north of west however, and after following it through pine and spruce country for 2½ miles [4 km] I branched south on another trail following up small stream.

Three miles up this I came to small lake in spruce muskeg country. The country rises gradually and another mile through pine [and a] few poplar, I made camp.

Milligan had crossed the summit as he estimated, but the summit hills are lower in the area east of where he had travelled the previous summer, and the summit was slightly further south.

The next day, he walked more than 30 kilometres and realized that he was on a main trail heading to Fort St John.

I passed over the summit yesterday without realizing it. I'm at least 30 miles [50 km] south of the country where I expected to meet Cartwright and haven't seen any evidence of his being in the country at all. I can't think what has happened to him. According to my estimated position on the map I'm between 80 and 100 miles [130–160 km] from Fort St John and have 2 days grub and 6 cartridges…. Light rain this evening necessitates putting up fly for first time since leaving Indian camp Sep 22nd.

On October 14 he followed a winding trail for about 25 kilometres that did not get him much farther south, but the next morning, he found the main trail again and followed it south. He walked more than 30 kilometres that day and when he made an observation on Altair that evening he found that he was about six kilometres north of the Dominion Block.

A Dunne-za family that Milligan met at the end of his 1914 exploration. BCA I-67826.

On October 16 Milligan finished his exploration, found Cartwright and heard news that would dramatically change his life.

> Tied my route survey to iron post on north boundary at about 9 this morning and continuing south about 10 miles [16 km] came to a Beaver Indian [Dunne-za] camp on the North Pine River. They told me that Cartwright was camped 5 miles to the southeast and I sent a couple of boys with word to him to come on to St John. The Indians also told me of a war between Germans and also forces of Britain, France, Russia.

The next day, he spent the morning at the Dunne-za camp reading about the war. Cartwright arrived at noon and the men each recounted their travels. Cartwright had got to the head of the Hay River, but too far east, into Alberta.

On the morning of October 18 Milligan and Cartwright left for Fort St John and arrived at the post the next day to find that the community had changed considerably.

> Where there was only several settlers when I left here in spring of 1913 there are now nearly 40 settlers on the plateau in the vicinity. I find that Mr [Frank] Beatton, the HB Manager is away and not expected back for several days. It is imperative that I meet him before I leave as I have two seasons' account to settle and also to arrange for the sale of our four horses. I will also be able to obtain boat from Mr Beatton.

Frank Swannell and his crew arrived the next evening. Swannell had been making a triangulation survey along the Finlay River. Like Milligan, he had not learned about the war in Europe until several weeks after it had

On the return trip, through Alberta. Milligan is in the back of the wagon. Frank Swannell photograph; BCA I-58386.

started, and he wanted to get back to Victoria as quickly as possible. He and Milligan arranged to go south together, taking the quickest route through Alberta.

While waiting for Beatton to return, Milligan went to Fred Hazen's homestead, about six kilometres away, to pick up some coal, iron and grass specimens that he had asked him to collect, and to take a few photographs of Hazen's oats and barley.

Swannell departed down the Peace River on October 23. Frank Beatton returned that evening. Milligan settled his accounts the following day and then also headed downstream. Swannell and his crew arrived at Dunvegan, a fur trading post on the Peace River in Alberta, on October 26, where they waited for Milligan and Cartwright, who arrived the following day. From there the two surveyors sent a telegram to the surveyor general. "Arrived here from headwaters Finlay River and Fort Nelson respectively. Swannell and Milligan." Three days later they reached Peace River Crossing. George Copley, Swannell's assistant, later recalled an incident that occurred there.

Don't forget the episode of Cartwright and his gallon jug of rum at
Peace River Xing. From what I remember he ordered the rum two years
before but it arrived in Peace River Xing after they had left to go north.

He told us all about it at Dunvegan and how we would enjoy it on our arrival at PR Xing. Shortly after we got there we went to the store and sure enough it was there OK with the HBC seal unbroken, so we took it up to his room, got hot water, sugar and glasses. Broke the seal and opened the jug. What a surprise, the jug was filled with water. It had been tapped on the way from Edmonton some way or other.

The men travelled for two days by wagon from Peace River Crossing to Lesser Slave Lake, where they boarded the *Northland Sun*, which took them to Sawridge. From there they took a train to Edmonton, arriving on November 3. The men spent two days in Edmonton before departing for Victoria, where they arrived on November 10.

E.B. Hart

At the beginning of the fall of 1914, E.B. Hart was on the upper Toad River. After receiving his January letter and report, Surveyor General George Dawson replied: "You will arrange to stop your exploration work next autumn, and you will have your final report, plans, etc., in this department not later than the middle of December. Presumably you will be returning to Victoria when the details of your exploration can be discussed, but should you be remaining in the north, you will please arrange to have full information in this department by the above mentioned date." After receiving Hart's June letter and report, Dawson wrote to him again on September 9:

> I have your report of the 21st of June, which I have read with very great interest, and I judge from contents that my letter to you of the 1st of April has not reached you, as I see you are planning to make your way to Edmonton in February next.
>
> It is my wish that you reached Victoria in sufficient time to enable a comprehensive report being published in the Annual Report of the department on the first day of January, which would be carefully scrutinized by both Mr Milligan and yourself, and should this letter reach you in time you will please amend your programme in order to allow your arriving in Victoria not later than the 1st of December.

Hart did not receive this letter either, but Dawson did not need to worry, because Hart was back in Victoria in November. In his final report Hart wrote:

> I had expected to find it [the upper Toad River] connected with the headwaters of the Finlay River, and it is possible that one of the minor forks may do so, but as there was six inches of snow on the ground, and in view of the fact that I had some two hundred miles [300 km] of canoe

travelling to do in order to get out of the country in the fall, and being near the end of September there was every danger of the ice beginning to run on the rivers (which would have rendered it impossible for me to get out). I was unable to determine this matter, and on the 22nd of September I started back down the Toad River to the Liard, thence by canoe down the Liard to the Fort Nelson River to Fort Nelson and overland to Fort St John, which point I reached on the 17th of October.

Hart arrived two days before Milligan and three before Swannell, but he did not remain at the post long enough to rendezvous with them. Instead, he built a raft and floated down to Peace River Crossing and from there made his way to Edmonton, where he sent the surveyor general a rush telegram. "Arrived Edmonton. No funds. Please wire one hundred and fifty dollars my credit Bank of Commerce Edmonton."

If Dawson had hoped that Hart would finish his report promptly and that Hart's expedition would conclude without further difficulties, he would be disappointed. On November 5 he received an invoice from the Hudson's Bay Company in Edmonton to cover a cash advance to Hart, and the next day a letter arrived, also from the HBC in Edmonton, containing invoices for freight and merchandise worth $304.11 "duly certified by Mr E.B. Hart." The company official explained: "While Mr Hart was at Fort Smith, he made arrangement with our Mr Brabant, for the Company to assume the balance of his supplies, those that he did not require. Unfortunately, however, he did not have the invoices covering the supplies at the time, so they could not arrive at the value, but as soon as Mr Brabant is in a position to value them, cheque will be sent to you." Because Hart did not have the invoice that listed the prices he paid for the supplies he was returning, the HBC charged the full amount and would issue a credit cheque later. On November 9 Dawson received a third letter from the HBC for supplies provided to Hart at Fort St John, followed the next day by an invoice for a cash advance of $50 to Hart.

The surveyor general replied on November 12: "It would be a convenience to this Department if, instead of sending a cheque for the supplies taken over by you from Mr Hart, you send a credit note, and the account thereof will be deducted from the total due you. Remittance for the account, however, is held over pending receiving the credit note referred to." The HBC official rejected his offer, saying, "as it will take considerable time before we can get credit note from the district manager at Fort Smith, I would be obliged if you would let us have cheque for the $304.11 and enable us to close out the account."

Dawson paid the other invoices but balked at this, the largest amount. "I regret that it is impossible for the Department to adopt your suggestion and pay the amount in full at the present time. You will readily understand that it will be an irregular proceeding for this bill to be paid in view of the fact that a certain amount of goods were not retained by Mr Hart. Mr Hart has been seen with reference to this matter, and he gives us a list of the actual goods which he retained, and a copy of this list is appended herewith. Perhaps this information will enable you to facilitate the proportion of the necessary credit."

In December the surveyor general received a bill of $2.05 from T.N. Hibben of Victoria for supplies sent to Hart in December 1913. Dawson replied, "I have the honour to inform you that this account should be paid by Mr Hart, and not by the Government."

Later that month he received another letter from the HBC:

The account for freight, however, is not affected by these circumstances, as when Mr Hart was here the difference in the freight rate between Fort Simpson, where the total consignment of goods was landed, and Fort Nelson, to which they were originally consigned was deducted from the account, and Mr Hart OK'd the account to Fort Nelson. As this freight account is altogether separate from the merchandise and belongs to a different department of the Company, I should be glad if you will have this amount of $116.38 passed for payment, as our Transport accounts for the year are being closed.

Dawson agreed to pay this amount.

In January 1915 the Wholesale Department of the HBC, based in Edmonton, sent an invoice to the surveyor general for supplies used by Hart, adding $8 for those given to him in August and an 85-cent freight charge for reshipping an item to Hart in Victoria Dawson sent the HBC's list of supplies to Hart, whose mailing address was the Union Club in Victoria. Hart replied, saying that he had returned four items, so the surveyor general asked the HBC to amend the invoice accordingly. He then approved payment in early February. The Wholesale Department thanked him for the payment but pointed out that he had forgotten to include the extra shipping charge of 85 cents.

Expense charges continued to arrive on the surveyor general's desk. On February 12 C.H. French, the HBC's district manager in Victoria, sent him a bill for $139.76 for expenses that Hart incurred at Fort Simpson. Dawson pointed out that this was the first he had heard of these expenses, but agreed to pay. He asked if he could include the small shipping charge in this payment, but the HBC wanted two separate cheques, one to Victoria and the other, the 85 cents, to Edmonton.

Dawson may have thought that he had finally concluded dealing with Hart's expenses, but there was still one more item. On September 7, 1915, he received an invoice for $240 from C.H. French. "I beg to enclose account in duplicate and certified by Corporal A.W. Joy of the Royal Northwest Mounted Police, covering supplies to Mrs Gardiner. These supplies were issued at the request of your Mr E.B. Hart, as per copy of his letter attached." Hart's letter, written on HBC stationery, was addressed to the manager of the Fort Simpson post and dated July 12, 1914. "Will you be so good as to pay Mrs Gardiner, wife of Archie Gardiner, through Corporal Joy, RNWMP, who has consented to act as agent for the above Archie Gardiner, the sum of $20.00 per month as rations for herself and her family, from the present date until the end of June 1915, and charge the same to the Surveyor General's Department, Victoria, BC."

Exasperated, Surveyor General Dawson replied on September 25:

I have to advise you that I have referred this matter to Mr Hart and will communicate with you further on the subject. I may say, however, that I am entirely at loss to understand Mr Hart's action in this matter. Mr Hart was employed by this Department during the years 1913–14 on an exploratory survey in northern BC. His employment terminated, however, early in November last.

The invoice clearly extended well beyond the time of Hart's employment, and Hart would have known that. On November 13 French sent another letter to Dawson inquiring about payment of this account.

Dawson did not know what to do about this invoice, so two days later he wrote a detailed letter to his superior, the minister of Lands.

I have the honour to request an expression of your wishes as to what action should be followed in connection with an account for $240.00 submitted by the Hudson's Bay Company and accompanied by an order signed by Mr E.B. Hart, who was employed by this Department during the years 1913 and 1914 in an exploratory expedition through northern British Columbia.

In so far as the employment of Mr Hart is concerned, I may say that toward the end of 1912 there was submitted to me an elaborate report on the extreme northern portion of the Province, prepared by Mr E.B. Hart, and for which he expected the government would pay the sum of $2,000.00. After some discussion with yourself I valued the report at $250.00 and signed a voucher for this amount. Early in 1913 Mr Hart applied to me for employment as an explorer. As I did not consider that the result of his exploration would be of any great value to the Department, I declined to employ him. Subsequently, however, I was directed to engage him for a period to include two working seasons, at the rate of $150.00 per month and his expenses, he to make a trip across the northern part of the Province and more particularly to make an examination of the extreme north-easterly portion. When handing him his instructions, I also gave him a letter to the Hudson's Bay Company, which, under the circumstances, was necessarily in the nature of a somewhat general order for assistance in the engaging of men and furnishing of supplies. A copy of this letter is herewith.

Mr Hart returned to Victoria later in the year 1914 and was paid up in full. He completed his field work early in November 1914, subsequently the order signed by him for payment of $20.00 per month to be made to Mrs Archie Gardiner extended for a period of nine months after the completion of his engagement by this Department.

The results of Mr Hart's exploration were, as I anticipated, found to be of no great value to this Department, and when making him his final payment I anticipated that this rather unfortunate incident was closed.

My reason for asking your decision as to how the claim of the Hudson's Bay Company should be dealt with, arises from the fact that it is frequently extremely convenient to this Department to avail itself of the privilege of making the credit of a surveyor in the north good at the stores of the Company, and that it will be unfortunate, if, through Mr Hart's action, the good understanding existing between the Company and myself be in any way disturbed.

I may say that this matter has been brought to Mr Hart's attention and that his explanation is most unsatisfactory. It is, briefly, that it was necessary for him to engage Gardiner and to provide for his wife in his absence: Gardiner remained in his employ for 5½ months, while his time for 3½ months only has been charged to the Department (vouchers substantiate that this was the time for which he was paid): that he forgot about Mrs Gardiner's order when field work closed down: that he disbursed so much of his own money in connection with his exploratory work that he is actually out of pocket.

I am given to understand that Mr Hart has no private means and that he has now enlisted for overseas service.

The incident resolves itself into making a decision as to whether is it advisable to pay the Hudson's Bay Company the amount of their claim, or advise them that no payment can be made for goods furnished after the 1st of November.

On January 20, 1916, French wrote another letter to Dawson reminding him that he had not responded to his letter in November. Dawson replied the next day stating that payment had been authorized. He also said:

In view of the many favours granted by your Company to surveyors in the employ of this Department in the past, I regret that there has been such a great delay in the settlement of your account. I would draw your attention, however, to the fact that the order on your Company, signed by Mr Hart on the 12th of July, 1914, was not brought to my attention until the 4th of September, 1915; and further, that I am of the opinion that Mr Hart had no right to issue such an order under his instructions received from me. The delivery of goods under this order would have been stopped by me had I been cognizant of its existence.

In a letter dated January 24, French had the final word, after thanking the surveyor general for the payment:

In explanation to the last paragraph of your letter I would say that as this order was given to cover the period between 12 July, 1914, to the end of June 1915, the account would naturally not be rendered until after the end of June 1915, and as Fort Simpson is in the Mackenzie district and mail facilities are not of the best, it is not surprising that we were not able to present this account before September 1915.

I would also say that the Hudson's Bay Company do not hold Mr Hart in very high esteem, and you can readily understand that they would not take any obligation of this kind until they felt sure that it was desired by the Government for them so to do.

In the Shadow of the Great War

In January 1915 F.C. Green (PLS #45), president of the BC Land Surveyors, addressed the organization's members at their annual gathering: "At our last meeting we little thought that the shadow of a great war would so soon cover our land in common with half the world. It is a time of great sacrifices and I know that most surveyors are doing all they can." He predicted correctly: "The bonanza years for surveyors have probably departed forever".

During the winter of 1914-15 William Cartwright and E.B. Hart completed their reports. Cartwright focused on the agricultural potential of the region, and he included photographs that Milligan had taken. He wrote about the geography of the region:

> In a general way the whole of this territory may be described as one huge
> plateau, except on its western limits where the country runs into small
> broken hills, which are undoubtedly the undulations from the foothills
> of the Rockies. Travelling north from the southern boundary, this plateau
> rises very gradually to a height of land dividing the water of the North
> Pine River from those of the Nelson River.... Inasmuch as there are no
> outstanding features to describe, there are also no points of vantage from
> which an idea of the general nature of the country can be obtained. This
> will be readily appreciated on reference to the photographs accompanying
> the detailed reports.

He recognized the importance of fire to the ecology of northeastern BC:

> The first impression on inspecting these plateau lands was not favourable.
> The month preceding our arrival on the ground exceptionally heavy rains
> had been falling, and owing to the flatness of the country (with conse-
> quent slow drainage), together with the clay subsoil, the whole district had
> the appearance of being in a flooded condition.
>
> On further travel and examination during the present summer, which
> the Indians state was more normal with regard to rainfall, it was found

that where fire had burnt off the overlaying covering of moss-like growth, allowing sun and air to reach the top soil, the lands had been in good heart to produce a fine growth of grass and vetches. On the other hand, and in spite of the more normal rainfall, the same wet conditions were still noticeable where fire had not visited the plateau. Towards the end of the summer, the moss becomes sufficiently dry to easily fire. Another feature on these plateau lands is a scattered growth of scrub spruce, which seldom exceeds 8 inches in diameter. After this growth has been burned, it would be a comparatively inexpensive matter to clear up the small down timber.

But, he cautioned, "if systematic firing is adopted on the plateau, the rights of the Indians would have to be taken into consideration".

Cartwright believed that the potential for farmland in the region would be primarily in raising livestock, because the "percentage of agricultural lands is small, compared with the range country". He felt that the cost of ranching would be "comparatively small, while the luxuriant growths along the river and creek bottoms suggests the ability to raise all the necessary winter feed, even for the long period this latitude demands." He noted that the chinooks in the western part of the area would "help considerably in wintering stock." He mentioned a few places where crops were being grown in the Fort Nelson drainage. "From what was seen, and the fact that the growing period is free from frost, it makes the outlook highly promising for the lands on the northern slope." `

In his summary Cartwright said:

The first and foremost necessity to bring this huge plateau country into use is modern transportation facilities. That portions of it can be made into a profitable territory is seen from the practical evidence already quoted. It is clearly demonstrated on the ground that burnt off areas pro- duce a fine grass crop, and therefore it would appear that systematic firing (together with a system of drainage) is one of the most pressing needs to bring this country to the forefront for stock raising.

But he pointed out the areas where he thought fire should not be used: "There is practically no timber of commercial value to lose on the plateau, although along the river bottoms the considerable growth of merchantable timber should be safeguarded, as it forms a considerable asset to the imme- diate adjoining country."

Cartwright was aware that the war would affect economic development in northeastern BC, and in his conclusion he wrote: "When the time is ripe for the developing and opening up of this territory, firing should take place prior to surveys and settlement."

Hart's report, just 35 double-spaced pages, summarized his travels through the area but contained no photographs. Large portions of this short docu- ment are similar to the reports he wrote to the surveyor general while he was in the field. Hart knew that the surveyor general wanted him to locate land that could be used for economic development, so whenever he found potential agricultural land or patches of merchantable timber Hart wrote enthusiastically about his observations. But his report mentions only a few of these places and contains no photographs of them.

Hart wrote about the Sekani and Dene-thah that he met in the area, stating that they appeared to be "rapidly dying off from tuberculosis and scrofula, and I fancy that there are not more than three hundred Indians all told in the two tribes."

Like Cartwright, Hart recognized the important role of fire in the ecology of the land and expected it to transform the landscape even further.

> In travelling over this wet country, especially with a heavy pack on one's
> back, one is apt to take rather a pessimistic view of its possibilities, but,
> viewed in the light of the changes which have occurred where fire has
> thoroughly swept the country and the moss has been dried off, one is
> forced to the conclusion that [more] great changes will take place in this
> country as have occurred.

He commented on his surveying difficulties:

> In travelling east from the mouth of the Dease River my watch became
> too erratic for accurate results in longitude and I was therefore compelled
> to use this point as a base after obtaining a more reliable time keeper. I have
> reason, however, for thinking that when a more accurate survey is made of
> the country, the position of this point will be found more to the east.

George Milligan submitted a preliminary report in December, enabling the surveyor general to publish some information about the exploration in his annual report for the year. Milligan delivered his final, detailed report in the spring of 1915. In the introduction he wrote: "The Fort Nelson country, owing probably to its inaccessibility and remoteness from the main lines of travel, has hitherto received but scant attention from explorers and travellers." He acknowledged William Ogilvie's quick survey through the area for the federal government in 1891 and the Klondikers who travelled through the area in 1898. He also mentioned, in the preceding few years, "the Treaty party of the Indian Department each summer made a trip across country from Fort St John to Fort Nelson.... Such considerable delay, however, was experienced each trip, owing to the amount of fallen timber, that this route has been abandoned."

Milligan calculated that during his 18 months in the field, between the time he left and returned to Edmonton, he had travelled 7211 kilometres. This included 2371 on foot, 1564 by pack horse, 819 by dogsled, and 716 by canoe, with the remainder by train, steamboat and wagon.

After defining the region of northeastern BC he explored, Milligan cautioned:

In stating that this area was mapped and explored, it is not to be understood that every part was actually visited, and there will no doubt be isolated patches of good land here and there not coming within our line of travel. Most of the main streams, however, were travelled, and different trips made across the plateau regions wherever practicable, and the data thus obtained, together with information gathered from the Indians, give a fairly good idea of the entire region included between the boundaries above mentioned.

He was unable to visit the Black River area in the extreme northeastern part of the province, so he relied on reports from others:

This country, according to information gathered from the Indians, is apparently similar in its physical aspects to that adjoining it on the south. As far as I could learn, there are no Indians now hunting in this region, excepting a few of the Fort Liard Indians, who travel some distance up the Black River from its mouth....

From one of the Dene-thah he learned that this watershed was a

region of scrub spruce and tamarac moss country....A large portion of the country has been visited by fires which, he said, spread north during the season the Klondikers passed through the country.

Milligan estimated that, in his area of exploration

about one quarter lies south of the summit and is drained by the North Pine River.... The main stream draining the northerly slope is the Fort Nelson River, flowing northwest into the Liard. The Hay River, flowing northeast into Great Slave Lake, also drains a portion of this area to the east.

In a general description of the region under review, one of the outstanding features is the uniformity of the surface....There is an absence of prominent hills and mountains, and although it is more or less undulating, the whole region may be spoken of as a huge plateau. Travelling north from the bench north of Peace River at an elevation of approximately 2100 feet [640 m], the country rises gradually to a height of land between the waters of the Peace and Fort Nelson Rivers. This watershed at the summit attains an altitude of approximately 3000 to 3700 feet [900–1100 m], and lies east and west across country at roughly latitude 57°30'. An excellent view of the territory to the north was obtained from this summit. Looking north and east, the country gradually subsides from its rough and broken character at the summit to that of low rounded ridges, and which as one proceeds north merge with the general level of the vast plateau which extends northerly through the country travelled.

The western boundary of the plateau region is formed by a line of broken flat-topped hills extending northwesterly between the Prophet and Fort Nelson Rivers. These hills are sharply defined and rise abruptly 1,000 feet [300 m] above the plateau, and would appear to have formed at one time part of a high table-land which extended easterly from the foothills of the Rockies.

In a section entitled "Moss and Muskeg", he described another important feature:

> With the exception of along the river valleys, the ground throughout
> this region is covered with a growth of moss varying in depth from a few
> inches to 6 feet. Our first summer in the country was unusually wet, and
> our first impression of these plateau lands was not favourable.... Upon
> further examination the following summer, which was dry and warm,
> these mossy areas seemed not so formidable. In warm dry weather the
> top of the moss is easily burnt, and large areas being swept by fire, a great
> change takes place: poplars and willows and grass grow where before was
> scrub spruce and tamarac. The moss acts as a sort of sponge and retains
> the moisture and keeps the heat of the sun out: in fact, there is ice on
> some of the muskegs year round.... There have been large tracts where
> the moss has been burnt out, and considerable burnt areas were encoun-
> tered that had previously been muskeg, as shown by patches of moss that
> were left where the muskeg had been. In this sort of burnt area grass was
> often found 2 to 4 feet [~1 m] high. When drained and the moss removed
> it is reasonable to suppose that the greater portion of this land will be
> cultivable.

Milligan singled out the North Pine watershed as having the best agricultural land in the area:

> On the plateau north of St John, included within the Peace River Block,
> are extensive areas of excellent land, and in comparison with the country
> travelled further north no areas were encountered to equal this in desir-
> ability from an agricultural point of view.... [Along the Blueberry River,
> just north of the Peace River Block,] are some excellent stretches of
> agricultural land, several townships of which have been surveyed by the
> Provincial Government and which are available for pre-emption. Good
> land is also found along the several streams shown flowing southerly paral-
> lel to the North Pine and emptying into the Blueberry.... [A large por-
> tion of the summit hills] would be available for summer range when the
> areas at present obstructed by windfalls, etc. are cleared off. Dotted along
> the summit are small clear lakes about the margin of which there is a thick
> growth of swamp hay.

He was not as optimistic about the area north of the summit. Some patches there had agricultural potential, but he also found large swampy sections, particularly as he travelled north.

> It was noted with regard to many of the streams in this flat country that
> the land immediately along the top of the benches is a few feet higher
> than the surrounding country, and although the drainage near the river is

William Cartwright (left) and an unknown companion on the timbered flats at the junction of the Muskwa and Fort Nelson rivers. Some of Milligan's photographs became useful for other government departments. This one appeared in *Forests of British Columbia*, a book published in 1918 by the Commission of Conservation Canada, as an example of forest land in the Fort Nelson region. LTSA.

general, back from the edge of the valley on the plateau there is usually a wide expanse of swamp covered by a stunted growth of spruce and tamarac and carpeted by heavy layers of moss. This description applies to large areas on the plateau to the north and south of Fontas River.

He wrote briefly about the timber in his area of exploration: "While practically the entire region is wooded, the only timber of merchantable value is found along the bottom of the valleys....The timber on the plateau is mostly scrub, principally ... good-sized spruce, pine, balsam and poplar: these are of no practical use." He had seen some stands of spruce trees along the banks of the North Pine, but cautioned that they "may not more than prove sufficient to meet the requirements of the district in the future". But he found a different situation in the Fort Nelson drainage:

On the north slope, however, for the entire length of the Fort Nelson River, and for a considerable distance up the Fontas and Sikanni [Chief] Rivers, is some of the finest spruce and cottonwood timber I have seen in the north. Although this timber extends seldom more than half a mile on either side from the rivers, it grows thickly and the trees are clean-trunked and tall.

Most of George Milligan's "Map of Northeasterly Portion of the Peace River District Compiled from Exploratory Surveys, 1913-1914". LTSA map 6, locker I. The original map is about 1 x 2 metres and shows Milligan's routes and campsites. It also shows the route of the Klondikers when they came through the area in

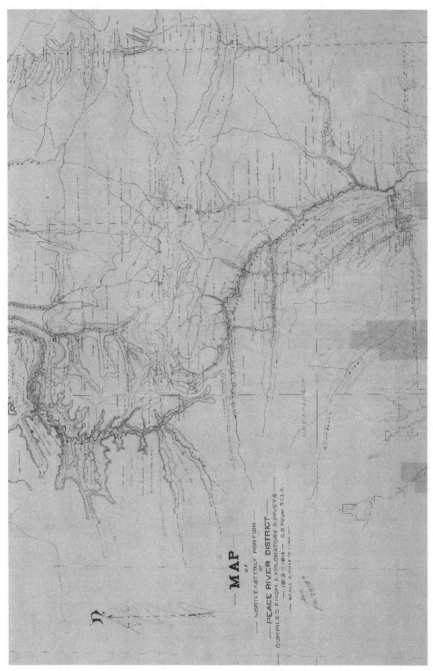

1898. Milligan used First Nations geographic names as much as possible, along with English translations. He did not have time to survey the land north of Kotcho Lake and left that part of the map almost blank, so it is not shown here.

Regarding minerals, "travelling across county over the plateau region, there was a marked absence of rock-exposures on the surface. What rock was seen was generally found along the rivers in places where the streams had cut into the sides of the valley." He found coal in the Sikanni Chief watershed and heard reports of coal seams in the area. "From these encouraging indications it is reasonable to suppose that systematic prospecting would result in demonstrating the existence of coal lands of economical and permanent value." He found no evidence of petroleum.

Milligan gave his impressions of the First Peoples of northeastern BC:

> North of the St John settlement there are no white settlers. There are no Indian villages such as are found west of the mountains. These Indians are nomads and travel and hunt in bands, with a chief selected from among themselves. The Beaver Indians [Dunne-za] who trade at Fort St John and Hudson Hope use horses and hunt as far north as the headwaters of the Fort Nelson River, and occasionally along the Upper Hay River. The Fort Nelson Indians are the Sikannie and Slaves [Dene-thah]. The former keep mostly to the west of the Fort Nelson River, while the Slaves hunt the country north and east and southeast of Fort Nelson.

> [The Dene-thah] live principally on moose meat and smaller game.... When an Indian party starts out from the post to their hunting ground, each member of the party, the children and dogs included, has to pack on his or her back part of the outfit. Their packs consist, besides their camp outfit, of principally tea and tobacco and cartridges. The hunters generally go ahead of the rest with an axe, rifle and light pack, and as soon as they arrive at the camping ground, leave their packs and go off on a hunt. It sometimes happens, when in a poor part of the country for moose, that they subsist for days entirely on a few rabbits and grouse, and sometimes squirrel.

Milligan concluded his report with a discussion of the climate of the area and included a 39-page chart with his daily weather record for the entire exploration.

In his annual government report written at the end of 1914, the surveyor general outlined the work done in the north. A brief section titled "Northern Exploration" mentioned the surveys of Frank Swannell and T.H. Taylor, and a section called "Peace River District" dealt with the Milligan and Hart explorations. Dawson described the Peace River District as "the portion of the province lying east of the Rocky Mountains, and which geographically would appear to belong rather to Alberta than to British Columbia, [which] has remained, to a large extent, unknown." Then he stated:

> With a view, however, of ascertaining the character of country and conditions existing in the north of the Dominion Block, an expedition was fitted out in the spring of 1913, and G.B. Milligan, together with a represen-

tative of the Agricultural Department, undertook an exploring trip which was to last eighteen months, or for two summers and one winter. Mr Milligan has recently returned, and while his final maps and report will not be ready in time to be incorporated with this, a preliminary report will be found attached hereto.

The geographical information obtained by Mr Milligan is of great interest, and will change the general appearance of the northeasterly corner of future maps of the Province in so far as the lakes and rivers are concerned. It seems that, speaking generally, the district north of the Dominion Railway Belt is a vast wooded or brush plain, with large areas of swamp and muskeg, and that where, as in the vicinity of rivers, the land has drainage, the soil appears to be good. It is gratifying to note that the report on the climate is satisfactory, particularly when the latitude of the district is taken into consideration.

E.B. Hart, who has spent many years in the northern part of the Province, has in the past eighteen months travelled from the mouth of the Stikine to the Peace River District and has spent over a year in the latter. Mr Hart's expenses were paid by this Branch and he was given a monthly allowance in consideration of his furnishing a report on the country explored. As Mr Hart returned to Victoria late in the year, his report is not available for publication.

The Department of Agriculture mentioned Cartwright's work and stated that his report "should prove of the utmost value to people who will be looking for reliable information as to land for settlement in the country before the Pacific Great Eastern Railway is completed".

By the time these reports were published the focus and finances of the government had turned toward the world war in Europe, and the information was filed away and forgotten. It was not until World War II and the construction of the Alaska Highway that the BC government once again focused attention on northeastern BC. The maps and reports made by Milligan and Hart were re-examined and used at the beginning of the Alaska Highway project and then put away. The last official government access of these records was in 1947.

The shadow of the Great War affected not only the results of these two explorations, but also the lives of the men who participated in them. Fred Hazen enlisted in the war and was killed in the Battle of the Somme. (J.R. Graham, who surveyed the townships north of the Peace River Block that Milligan used to begin his exploration and worked with Milligan in the Halfway River valley in 1912, also died in the fighting around the Somme.) William Cartwright was severely wounded by a sniper's bullet that shattered his jaw and struck him in the shoulder. He survived and after the war became a Conservation officer, but he never returned to northern BC.

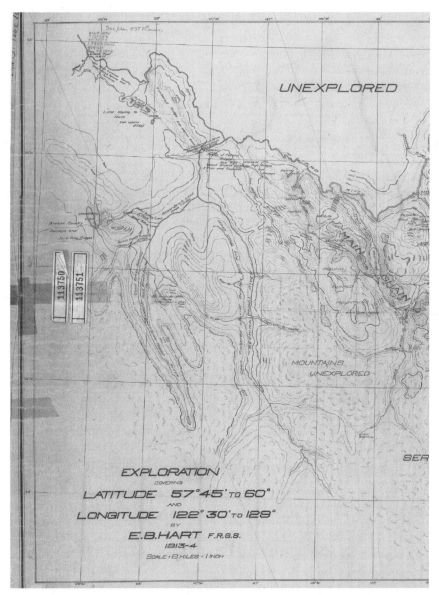

E.B Hart's map, "Exploration Covering Latitude 57°45' to 60° and Longitude 122°30' to 129°". LTSA 5T169.

The orignal map is about 50 x 100 centimetres. The scale is eight inches per mile, compared to four per mile in Milligan's map, and is not as detailed. Hart based this map on his travels in the area from 1912 to 1914, and it includes some of his routes. Like Milligan, he used First Nations geographic names wherever possible – the legend includes First Nations equivalents for lakes and other waterways.

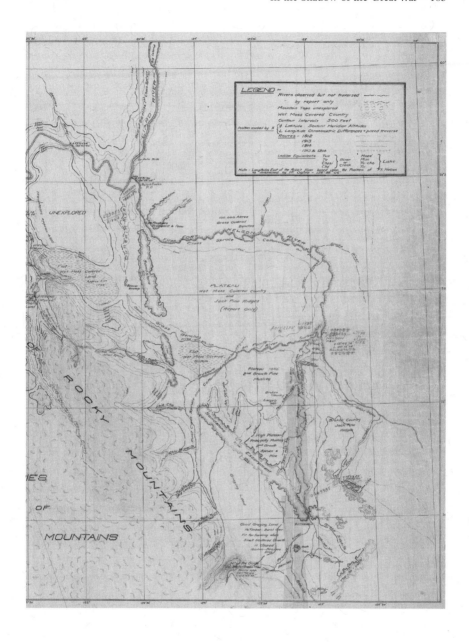

George Milligan joined the British army in 1915 and served in the Royal Field Artillery. He died on March 24, 1918, in France during the first days of the German spring offensive. The BC Land Surveyor's Roll of Honour states: "For his service in the field, he was twice mentioned in Dispatches and recommended for the Distinguished Service Order and Military Cross." J.H. Gray wrote a tribute to his former apprentice and partner for the Victoria *Daily Colonist* on April 2:

> The death of G.B. Milligan, BCLS, native son, explorer, athlete and all-round fine fellow marks not only an irreparable gap in his chosen profession, but a loss to the community, probably not manifested on account of his reticent nature, through the development of provincial resources, of which he possessed wide knowledge and in which he seemed destined to take a leading part.

The war had a profound effect on the Milligan family. George's younger brother, Alexander, the lawyer, also died in the war. His oldest brother, John, was gassed at the Battle of Ypres, captured by the Germans and spent more than three years in prison. The ordeal affected his health and he died at age 40. The fourth brother, who also fought in the war, suffered from post-traumatic stress disorder for the rest of his life. A sister who was engaged to a soldier killed in the war never married.

E.B. Hart also served in World War I. On his attestation paper he listed his occupation as explorer. Even though he was in his forties, Hart was accepted, probably because he was a Boer War veteran. He enlisted as a captain at the beginning of 1916 and was sent overseas where he participated in several battles. In November 1916 he received the Military Cross. His citation stated: "For conspicuous gallantry in action. He assumed command in the front line, and maintained his position at a very critical time, displaying great courage and determination. Later, he rendered most valuable services as an intelligence officer." He was promoted to the rank of major.

In the spring of 1918 Hart narrowly avoided being killed during the Battle of Arras. A report stated that he "was in brigade support in front of Arras on morning of April 29th. Shell burst in part of the shelter and fragment of shell case struck him in scalp – right side vertex above origin of temporal muscle making an irregular wound. X-ray says no injury to bone." The report noted that he had a concussion and a wound 13 centimetres long, but fortunately the fragment only grazed his skull. He eventually made a full recovery and, by August, returned to active duty. He was posted to the Allied expedition in Russia and sent to Murmansk as an intelligence officer. He remained there until the summer of 1919 and returned to Canada at the beginning of September.

E.B. Hart spent most of his remaining years in Williams Lake. He served as a stipendiary magistrate for more than 20 years he and was actively involved with the Williams Lake Golf and Tennis Club. Hart maintained an interest in the ethnography of First Nations in northern BC. In 1928, after making a survey that covered the Prophet River area, Dominion land surveyor Knox McCusker proposed to change the name Wahthinli Mountain to Mount Olympus for the new map sheet. When he heard this information Hart wrote a letter to G.G. Aitken, the BC government's chief geographer.

> I hope you will protest against any change being made in the name which I gave it. I fail to see either the necessity or advisability of giving Greek names to any of our mountains or natural features. The Greeks had their gods and their mountains sacred to them. Our natives equally had their gods and their sacred mountains. I have given it their native name....
> I feel rather strongly in this matter. The mountain is a most spectacular feature and in years to come will be one of the most famous in the whole Rocky chain.

Before receiving this letter Aitken had found the information that Hart had submitted regarding Wahthinli Mountain in 1915 and he informed the Geographical Board of Canada. The secretary noted that there was a convenient solution to the situation. "I find that Mt Olympus lies just outside the boundary of Prophet River sheet on topographical survey, so that the name will not appear on the map." After receiving Hart's letter Aitken forwarded it to the Secretary. "Major Hart's letter should be retained as a record of discovery, report and defining the English meaning of the word – Mountain of the Gods."

Aitken began his reply to Hart with, "Dear Major, I was very pleased to get your letter of the 26th November and to learn that you are well and going strong." After informing him that the mountain's name would remain Wahthinli, Aitken closed with an invitation: "When you are making your next visit to Victoria, I hope we may have a chat together again upon our maps and mapping."

McCusker, who was a trail guide as well as a surveyor, took the Mary Henry family through the Prophet River area in 1931 and made a sketch map at that time. Following this trip McCusker proposed to name several features in the area after members of the Henry family. Almost all of these geographic locations were First Nations names that Hart had submitted in 1915. BC's surveyor general, F.C. Green, wrote to his federal counterpart in Ottawa, saying "we propose to maintain Mr Hart's naming which, though not submitted to the Board, has been generally used and accepted here". Canada's surveyor general, F.H. Peters, readily concurred.

G.G. Aitken wrote to Mary Henry, explaining why Hart's names were retained, noting "[Hart] was particularly keen on ethnological data, and so made careful effort to obtain and record the Indian naming ... for the various geographical features in his area."

While Hart's geographical names were worth defending, his maps had much less value. In 1930 Bill and Ruth Albee came from California and travelled by themselves through the northern wilderness from Prince George to Alaska. They wrote about their experience in a book called *Alaska Challenge*. While trying to locate a map of the northern Rocky Mountain Trench a government official gave them a copy of Hart's map "with the cheery prediction that it wasn't worth the paper it was printed on.... We could, if we liked, talk with the man who had drawn the thing. He was living at a small settlement along the road to Prince George, and if we were going that way...." So, the Albees visited Hart at Williams Lake.

> We found Colonel Jones – which incidentally, wasn't his name – a precise little man, and irresistibly eloquent, once roused from the feather bed where he had been dozing the forenoon away in luxurious pink silk pyjamas.
>
> He was delighted to see us and explain the map work of his younger days. He called our attention to several outstanding details, particularly to an Indian trail which, he assured us, led the last hundred miles straight into Liard Post. We would pick it up at the base of a forty-mile [65-km] ridge. We couldn't miss the ridge. Nothing else like it in that part of the country. See? There it was, marked clearly: "Timbered Ridge. Elevation approx. 4000 feet [1200 m].
>
> Completely sold on the Colonel, we thanked him effusively.

From Summit Lake, north of Prince George, the Albees followed the Rocky Mountain Trench north, going up the Finlay River valley and crossing Sifton Pass into the Kechika River valley that Hart had visited in 1912 and 1913. The Albees found walking slower than they anticipated, so they built a raft and travelled down the river until it became too swift for them. Then they resumed walking. "We can't possibly miss that ridge. The Colonel said there's nothing like it in this part of the country. And the blueprint says it's right over there." The Albees didn't find the trail to Lower Post and got lost in the northern Kechika River valley. One day they climbed a high ridge and spotted the Rockies far to the northeast.

> We spread out the blueprint on a big stone and tried calmly, methodically, to orient ourselves: tried to imagine some connection between the forty mile ridge promised so definitely by Colonel Jones and this rolling timberland stretching mile on mile as far as we could see.
>
> Scanning the map once more, my eyes rested on the neatly lettered legend. I read aloud, "Timbered ridge. Elevation approx. 4000 feet."
>
> Approximately four thousand – four thousand –
>
> Suddenly the truth struck home. I saw in a flash what a fool I was for not having discovered it weeks before. Because the truth was – and I'd known it all along but never thought – the truth was that nowhere in all

that country did timber ever grow in altitudes higher than about three thousand feet. There could be no such timbered ridge as our blueprint showed. It was faked!

Fortunately for the Albees, while they were pondering their situation, a First Nations man came by the base of this hill and rescued them.

Despite the inaccuracies in Hart's map, it was the most accurate government map of that portion of BC until the 1940s. The Mary Henry expedition used Hart's map when they travelled through the area in 1931. When the Alaska Highway came through the upper Liard they also used Hart's map at the beginning of the road construction.

E.B. Hart died in 1948 and is buried in an unmarked grave at Williams Lake.

The Milligan and Hart explorations had many accomplishments. They provided the first maps of northeastern British Columbia; George Milligan's map, especially, was very accurate and detailed. Both men used the First Nations names for the geographical features wherever possible. Both men, particularly Milligan, provided extensive meteorological data that can be used for climate change comparison today. Milligan and Hart also produced some of the earliest detailed written records of the way of life of the three First Nations groups who lived in this remote boreal forest area of northeastern BC. Both expeditions gave information about the economic resources of the area, and both had an understanding of the role of fire in the ecology of the landscape.

William Cartwright gathered extensive, detailed information about the agricultural potential of the region. E.B. Hart collected plants that are still studied by scientists. The clothing items that he acquired are housed today in the Smithsonian Institution and are among the oldest surviving garments from the Fort Nelson area. Milligan's photographs provide the first detailed record of the landscape, along with the earliest pictures of the First Nations people who lived there. His diary provides a window into life in one of BC's most remote regions in the early 1900s and shows that he was a talented, skilled surveyor. But all of these accomplishments were overshadowed by the Great War.

Today the Major Hart River, in the Kechika drainage, and Milligan Creek, Milligan Hills, and Milligan Hills Provincial Park, all in the area Milligan surveyed in 1913 and 1914, commemorate these two important explorations that occurred a century ago.

Acknowledgements

First and foremost I thank Janet Mason, provincial topynomist, for locating the information that led to the discovery of the Hart and Milligan files, and Calvin Woelke of the Land Title Survey Authority for actually finding this material. Thanks also to Deputy Surveyor General Jeff Beddoes for arranging permission to use this material.

Once again, I thank the staff in the Reading Room at the BC Archives for their assistance, particularly Claire Gilbert. My appreciation also goes to the staff of the Hudson's Bay Company Archives for their assistance while I was in Winnipeg. Dan Savard helped me locate the Milligan photos in the Ethnology Collection of the Royal BC Museum. Jennifer Coupe from the Fort Nelson First Nations office provided the biographical information that her office had gathered about some of their elders. My thanks to Randy Bouchard for sharing his information about the Dunne-za and Dene-thah First Nations people. Judy Hawthorne from the North Peace Museum helped with the Frank Beatton journals. William Cartwright's son, Jim, provided information about his father. Ross Peck shared his knowledge of the people and places in the region explored by Milligan and Hart.

I thank my wife for her assistance with another book and the Royal BC Museum for publishing this book.

Sources Consulted

Archival Material

Land Title Survey Authority: Surveyor General's Vault
Hart, E.B.
  File 6952A – Cassiar 1912.
  File 6952S – Northern BC, 1913-14.
  File 7229 – Northern BC, 1913-14, expenses.
  Map 5T169 – "Exploration Covering Latitude 57°45' to 60° and
    Longitude 122°30' to 129°, 1913-1914".
  "Report on Surveys in the Cassiar District" in *Report of the Survey
    Branch of the Department of Lands*, 1912, pp. 49-52.
Milligan, G.B.
  Diary 1912.
  Diary 1913-14.
  File 3418 – Halfway River, 1912.
  File 7919S – Northeastern BC, 1913-14.
  File 8741– Northeastern BC, 1913-14, expenses.
  Map 6 Locker I – "Map of Northeasterly Portion of the Peace River
    District Compiled from Exploratory Surveys, 1913-1914".

BC Archives
Beatton, Frank Wark. Diaries 1911-14. MS 749.
BC Department of Mines. Gold Commissioner 1873-1931, Cassiar. GR
  0218.
BC Magistrate's Court, Williams Lake, 1923-1950. GR-0026.
BC Provincial Police Force, Telegraph Creek: Record of Arrivals and
  Departures, 1909-20. GR3046.

Cartwright, William H. "Report on the physical features, soil conditions and agricultural possibilities of the northeastern section of the province, 1914". C/D/30.9 C24.

Ogilvie, William. *Report on the Peace River and its Tributaries in 1891.* Ottawa: Queen's Printer, 1892. NW972.17Y94.

Swannell, Frank. Diaries 1913, 1914. MS 392.

Library and Archives Canada

Soldiers of the South African War – Hart, Ethelbert, RG38: (Volume 131), (a-1a, vol. 44); RG 9, II-A-5, vol. 13.

World War I – Hart, Major Edward Burton, RG150. Accession 1992-93/166, Box 4117-2.

Hudson's Bay Company Archives

B226/b/53.4 – Cassiar District subject file correspondence.

B226/b/54 – British Columbia district letter register 1908-09.

D38/8-44 – Departmental and district staff records.

D38/42 – British Columbia district staff records.

City of Vancouver Archives

MSS 505 – John Davidson fonds.

BC Government: Provincial Toponymist Office

File P.1.28, File S.1.36.

Libraries and Museums

Atlin Historical Museum

"Henry Esson Young file".

Beaty Biodiversity Museum, Vancouver, BC

E.B. Hart plant collection.

British Columbia Legislative Library

Hart, E.B. *Report on Exploration in Northeastern British Columbia 1913-1914,* "New British Columbia". Official Bulletin No. 22. Bureau of Provincial Information. Victoria: King's Printer, 1912.

Hudson's Hope Museum

"Donald MacDonald file".

National Museum of the American Indian, Smithsonian Institution, Washington, DC
E.B. Hart collection 15/4648 – 15/4653.

Sessional Papers

Government of British Columbia
Sessional Papers. First Session, Thirteenth Parliament.
    Dawson, G.H. "Report of the Surveyor General", pp. D225-39.
    Milligan, G.B. "Peace River Valley of Halfway River", pp. D299-300.
Sessional Papers. Third Session, Thirteenth Parliament.
    Dawson, G.H. "Report of the Surveyor General", pp. D49-61.
    Milligan, G.B. "Exploration Survey in Peace River District",
        pp. D90-95.
    Scott, W.E. "Deputy Minister of Agriculture Report", p. R63.
Sessional Papers. Fourth Session, Thirteenth Parliament.
    Milligan, G.B. "Exploratory Survey North of the Peace River Block",
        pp. B117-70.

Government of Canada
Sessional Paper 35a, 1903, Appendix F – Second Canadian Mounted
    Rifles.
Sessional Paper 27, 1912 – Report of H.A. Conroy, Inspector,
    Treaty 8.

Books

Albee, Ruth, and Bill Albee. *Alaska Challenge*. New York: Dodd, Mead &
    Company, 1940.
Campbell, Isabel M., ed. *Pioneers of the Peace*. Grand Prairie, Alberta:
    Grande Prairie and District Old Timers' Association, 1975.
MacGregor, J.G. *The Klondike Rush Through Edmonton, 1897–98*. Toronto:
    McClelland and Stewart, 1970.
Murray, Peter. *Home from the Hill: Three Gentlemen Adventurers*. Victoria:
    Horsdal & Schubart, 1994.
Patterson, R.M. *The Dangerous River*. Sidney, BC: Gray's Publishing, ca
    1966.
Patterson, R.M. *Trail to the Interior*. Toronto: McMillan, 1966.
Ventress, Cora, Marguerite Davies and Edith Kyllo. *The Peacemakers of
    North Peace*. Privately published, 1973.

Newspaper and Magazine articles

The Daily Colonist, Victoria
"Victoria Party to Peace River", May 8, 1913, pp. 1, 14.
"Peace River Country", Nov. 18, 1914, p. 7.
"Fellow Surveyor Pays a Tribute", April 2, 1918, p. 5.

Popular Mechanics
"Orchids found in far north in steam-heated valley". January 1926,
p. 103.

Index

Jay Sherwood

From 1979 to 1986, Jay Sherwood lived and taught school in Vanderhoof. There, he learned about the legendary land surveyor, Frank Swannell through his involvement with the local history society. A former surveyor, himself, Sherwood embarked on a study of Swannell that would result in the publication of three books about him. While researching Swannell's work, Sherwood uncovered a memoir written by Bob White (1902–85), a cowboy and packer who worked on the Bedaux Expedition, in which Swannell played a small part. He transcribed White's account, edited it and wrote a contextual framework for the story.

Jay Sherwood recently retired from his teaching position in Vancouver to concentrate on his historical research projects. His interest in land surveyors led him to write *Furrows in the Sky* and this book.

Other Books by Jay Sherwood:

Surveying Northern British Columbia: A Photojournal of Frank Swannell (Caitlin Press 2005)

Surveying Central British Columbia: A Photojournal of Frank Swannell, 1920–1928 (Royal BC Museum 2007)

Bannock and Beans: A Cowboy's Account of the Bedaux Expedition (Royal BC Museum 2009)

Return to Northern British Columbia: A Photojournal of Frank Swannell, 1929–1939 (Royal BC Museum 2010)

Furrows in the Sky: The Adventures of Gerry Andrews (Royal BC Museum 2012)

The Royal BC Museum

British Columbia is a big land with a unique history. As the province's museum and archives, the Royal BC Museum captures British Columbia's story and shares it with the world. It does so by collecting, preserving and interpreting millions of artifacts, specimens and documents of provincial significance, and by producing publications, exhibitions and public programs that bring the past to life in exciting, innovative and personal ways. The Royal BC Museum helps to explain what it means to be British Columbian and to define the role this province plays in the world.

The Royal BC Museum administers a unique cultural precinct in the heart of British Columbia's capital city. This site incorporates the Royal BC Museum (est. 1886), the BC Archives (est. 1894), the Netherlands Centennial Carillon, Helmcken House, St Ann's Schoolhouse and Thunderbird Park, which is home to *Wawadiła* (Mungo Martin House).

Although its buildings are located in Victoria, the Royal BC Museum has a mandate to serve all citizens of the province, wherever they live. It meets this mandate by: conducting and supporting field research; lending artifacts, specimens and documents to other institutions; publishing books (like this one) about BC's history and environment; producing travelling exhibitions; delivering a variety of services by phone, fax, mail and e-mail; and providing a vast array of information on its website about all of its collections and holdings.

From its inception 125 years ago, the Royal BC Museum has been led by people who care passionately about this province and work to fulfil its mission to preserve and share the story of British Columbia.

Find out more about the Royal BC Museum at
www.royalbcmuseum.bc.ca